Backcountry Banff

Walking, hiking, backpacking, and off-trail scrambling in Banff National Park

Mike Potter

LUMINOUS
COMPOSITIONS

IMPORTANT SAFETY NOTE: Those who participate in the activities described in this guidebook must be prepared for risks and must know how to evaluate them in order to proceed safely. See the Safety section, pages 19-26.

Backcountry
Banff

Mike Potter

Published by
Luminous Compositions
P.O. Box 909
Turner Valley, Alberta
Canada T0L 2A0

e-mail: luminous@telusplanet.net

Canadian Cataloguing in Publication Data

Potter, Mike, 1954-
   Backcountry Banff

Includes index.
ISBN 0-9694438-1-1

1. Trails—Alberta—Banff National Park—Guide-books.
2. Hiking—Alberta—Banff National Park—Guide-books.
3. Backpacking—Alberta—Banff National Park—Guide-books.
4. Banff National Park (Alta.)—Guide-books.
I. Title
GV199.44.C22B356 1992   917.123'32   C92-091127-7

Printed and bound in Canada by
Friesens Corporation
P.O. Box 720
Altona, Manitoba
Canada R0G 0B0

All photographs by Mike Potter.
Front cover: The author looking over Aylmer Pass to Mt. Aylmer.
Back cover: Backpacker at Howard Douglas Lake on *Citadel Pass* trail in autumn with golden larches.
Title pages: The author looking over ridge with site of former Aylmer fire lookout tower to Lake Minnewanka.
Contents: The author approaching the backcountry campground on the *Elk Pass* trail.

Foreword to Original Edition

One thousand kilometres of trails in Banff National Park? You bet; probably more. And that's counting only the main trails, the ones Parks Canada looks after. The others are kept open by the elk, the moose and the bighorn sheep—at no cost to the taxpayer.

Mike Potter has hiked practically all the park's established paths, and he's scrambled over countless logs and across dozens of scree slopes along the other kind. Mike has learned a great deal about navigating Banff's small sea of peaks, and it's all here, in this book, ready to go with you on your own adventures. Rely on Mike's book; it's just as good as his first trail guide, *Hiking Lake Louise*.

I read the manuscript for this book in the winter. It made me hungry for the summer as I word-walked with Mike through the Whistling Valley and over Pipestone Pass and up Cascade Mountain and down the switchbacks to Marvel Lake. Trail guides are books of dreams. You read them and plan. Come summer, you go.

As you go, consider this: the whole world once looked this way. The landscape was laced together with trails, not roads. Banff National Park preserves a fair-sized patch of the primitive, and some of us—people like Mike and me, and perhaps you, dear reader—can't live without it. I think we crave the wilderness because the human species grew up in it. Our bodies are built for the forests and the boulderfields; our minds carry ancient memories from the middle of nowhere. We're happy out there, even when the rain is turning to snow and the wind is coming up and the bear crap is so fresh that it's still steaming. Incredibly, we *enjoy* this kind of thing.

Well, now we can enjoy it with a new friend: Mike Potter's book. Happy hiking.

— Ben Gadd, Jasper, February 4, 1992

Mt. Cory and meadow from extension of *Muleshoe* trail.

Acknowledgements for 2001 Edition

I am most appreciative of the assistance given to me by many people while I was working on this book.

Ben Gadd of Jasper was of great help as editor of the original edition, both because of his command of the language and because of his deep understanding of the Canadian Rockies. Ben wrote the evocative foreword to this book.

Perry Davis and Don Gorrie of Banff National Park proved patient and knowledgeable sources of information on the park's network of trails.

Andre Dmytriev, supervisor of Parks Canada's Banff Visitor Centre, gave many useful comments in his review of the original manuscript and answered more questions for this edition.

Jeff Waugh of the park commented on interpretive information.

Many Banff National Park wardens provided assistance: Tim Auger, Reg Bunyan, Frank Burstrom, Mike Comeau, Larry Gilmar, Bob Haney, Anders Hawkins, Tom Hurd, Gord Irwin, Rick Kunelius, Don Mickle, Glen Peers, Ian Pengelly, Terry Skjonsberg, Cyndi Smith, Diane Volkers, Don Waters, Cliff White, and Chris Worobets.

Other park staff who contributed include Pierce Achtymichuk, Doug Brown, and Judy Otton.

Mary Andrews, Lena Goon, and Alex Huculak of the Archives, Whyte Museum of the Canadian Rockies, Banff, provided cheerful and efficient service with research.

Scott Morgan of the now-closed Banff Weather Office gave climate data, and Doug McKown gave background on lightning.

Dr. Valerius Geist provided details on mineral licks, Martin Jalkotzy gave information on cougars, while the late Jim Deegan and the late Bill Vroom recollected the history of Cuthead College.

Anthony Neilson of Deltaform Publications gave pre-press advice for the 2001 edition.

Finally, I'd like to thank Peter Duck, whose six-week backpacking trip in the backcountry of Banff National Park in 1985 was an inspiration to me to get out there.

Notwithstanding all the above generous involvment, I alone am responsible for any errors in this book. If you find any, please write to me at P.O. Box 909, Turner Valley, Alberta, Canada T0L 2A0, or send an e-mail to: luminous@telusplanet.net

I dedicate this book to my mother and my father, who awakened and encouraged my interest in the natural world.

Preface to 2001 Edition

My first experience of hiking in Banff National Park came over 30 years ago. It was when I started work there as a park interpreter in 1986, however, that I began in earnest to explore the region. The summer of 1990, during which I took a leave of absence from my park position, was a glorious opportunity to go on several long backpacking excursions into the more remote areas of the park.

I have left Parks Canada, and Banff too (in 1999), but I still get out there as much as possible, whatever the season and the circumstances. Whether sauntering along a short trail or venturing into the backcountry, there is a sense of renewal, a feeling of revitalization, in savouring the subtleties and the splendours of our naural surroundings.

I have shared my feelings about and my knowledge of the park with outdoor enthusiasts in five other books (including my *Hiking Lake Louise* trail guide), with visitors as part of my Parks job, with readers of the *Banff Crag & Canyon* newspaper in my former "Backcountry Banff" column, and with many others in freelance articles and photographs.

My wish is that these insights and this information will be apparent in this book, and that **Backcountry Banff** will prove useful and helpful in developing and cultivating a sense of this wonderful multi-faceted place.

Banff National Park encompasses much of enduring interest and provides ample scope to engage in adventure. I hope you enjoy its richness.

Mike Potter
June, 2001

South ridge of Cirque Peak above Helen Lake.

Contents

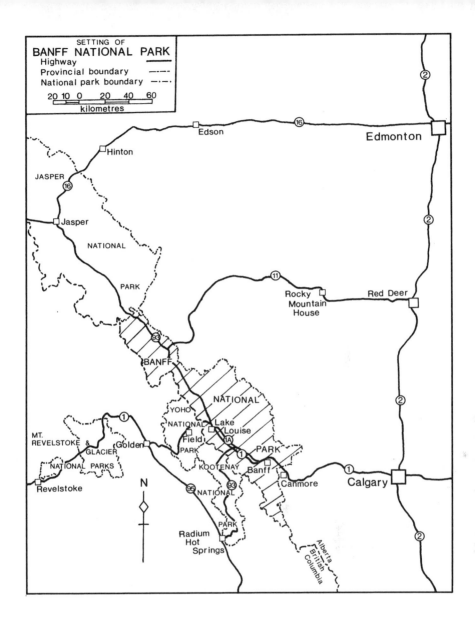

SETTING OF
BANFF NATIONAL PARK
Highway
Provincial boundary
National park boundary

20 10 0   20   40   60
kilometres

Introduction

Banff National Park is distinguished as one of Earth's great protected areas, a tribute recognized by its inclusion in a World Heritage Site. Although transportation corridors and population centres fall within its 6641 square kilometre territory, the park nonetheless offers many rewarding walks, hikes, backpacks, and off-trail scrambles.

The wilderness within Banff National Park shelters and supports a wide variety of wildlife and plants. It encompasses the range of the Canadian Rockies' inspiring landscapes, from towering mountains to tiny tarns. The story of the park includes tales of colourful characters and extraordinary exploits.

This guidebook invites you to experience firsthand the many aspects of this fascinating area by venturing onto some of the more than 1100 kilometres of trails described. On the following pages are found an overview of general information for the outings, then on p. 30 begin the comprehensive descriptions of individual trails.

Enjoy, appreciate, and pass on your enthusiasm for the intrinsic qualities of this wildscape...all the while keeping any damage to an absolute minimum. Like many other things, there's an apprenticeship of sorts to outdoor travel; a progression occurs while learning about and doing these activities. Mary Schäffer's experience is indicative—of an early overnight trip, she wrote that she "looked out upon [a] magnificent scene [but] with chattering teeth and shivering body, and vowed never again to camp in the Canadian Rockies." However, she persisted and became so accomplished that the Native Stoney people called her *Yahe-Weha*, "Mountain Woman." She later wrote of having "learned the secret of comfort, content, and peace on very little of the world's material goods, learned to value at its true worth the great un-lonely silence of the wilderness."

North down Peters Creek.

Using This Guidebook

The trails and routes of Banff National Park fall into five sections, beginning with those near Banff townsite. Flowing clockwise from there, the other four sections cover the south sector of the park, the area from Citadel Pass to Bow Summit that lies west of major roadways, the north end of the park, and its large east-central territory.

(This book—for reasons of length and thus cost—does not cover the Lake Louise area, which is described in *Hiking Lake Louise*: available in bookstores and outdoor equipment outlets or by mail from the publisher. [See copyright info on p. 4 for postal and e-mail addresses.])

The name of each trail described in **Backcountry Banff** comes from its destination or its most prominent feature. The overall distance between specified beginning and end points is given in kilometres (km) and miles (mi).

Each outing is in one of the following four categories:

— a **walk** is short, with little or no elevation gain: such an outing will appeal if time is limited or if looking for a relaxing stroll;

— a **day hike** varies from a jaunt of a couple of hours to an excursion taking most of a summer day, and entails some or considerable elevation gain;

— a **backpack** usually involves multi-day backcountry travel, although many backcountry campgtounds can be reached in a day and used as bases for day hikes (the hybrid category **day hike/backpack** indicates a trail that can be taken as a day hike or as part of a backpacking trip);

— an **off-trail scramble** goes off or beyond established, maintained trails.

Note that to attempt an off-trail scramble requires good routefinding skills, including map-and-compass navigation where necessary. Equipment has to be in good condition. Travel on steep snow slopes calls for an ice axe and the ability to perform a self-arrest in case of an out-of-control slide toward a cliff or jagged rocks. Other terrain negotiated on off-trail scrambles includes scree, boulderfields, trackless forest, and featureless alpine meadows. On all scrambles, it is essential to keep impact to a minimum.

After the category for each decription is an estimate of the time necessary to cover each trail or route at an average pace, one way (unless a loop) in the distance described. The estimate is for actual hiking time; extra time should be allowed for rest breaks, snacks or lunch, photography, and nature observation.

Descending a trail with lots of elevation gain clearly takes less time than the ascent; dividing the outbound estimate by two, or by three if the trail is very steep, will give an idea of the time required to get down.

The elevation gain or loss on each trail or route is given in metres (m) and feet (ft). For outings where there is a lot of up and down, the figures are cumulative totals.

The maximum elevation is given in metres and feet.

The map (or maps) required for each trail is (are) noted, first the excellent ones produced by Gem Trek Publishing {(403) 932-4208; www.gemtrek.com}, then those in the National Topographic System [NTS] of 1:50,000 scale topo sheets.

Trailhead info follows next: the start of each trail or route is usually a parking area, or at a specified distance along a previous description. There are trailhead kiosks (small shelters with maps and information) at the beginning of many trails.

A synopsis of each trail or route provides:

— the cumulative distance in kilometres at intermediate junctions and important features such as backcountry campgrounds;

— the elevation in metres at the beginning, significant intermediate points, and the end;

— the direction to be taken at junctions in order to reach the destination, and where the other direction leads;

— the physical characteristics of the trail (e.g., level, gradual, steep; wide, narrow; well-established, faint); and

— mention of connecting trails and routes.

The body of each description gives information on features found along the trail, such as the surrounding landscape and nearby peaks, as well as natural history lore including flora and fauna, geology, and glaciology. Anecdotes of human history leaven the mix.

Access

Banff National Park is readily accessible, although some parking area trailheads can be difficult to reach using public transportation.

The Trans-Canada Highway (Highway 1) passes through the west-central area of the park. Banff townsite is 138 km (86 mi) west of Calgary and 82 km (51 km) southeast of the Yoho National Park community of Field, British Columbia. The Trans-Canada continues west to the town of Golden, Glacier and Mount Revelstoke national parks, Kamloops, and ultimately Vancouver and Victoria.

The Banff-Windermere Parkway (Highway 93 South) leads southwest from Castle Junction through Kootenay National Park to Radium Hot Springs and the Rocky Mountain Trench.

The Icefields Parkway (Highway 93 North) runs northwest from Lake Louise to Jasper townsite in 233 km (144 mi), passing out of Banff National Park into Jasper National Park at Sunwapta Pass just south of the toe of the Athabasca Glacier.

The David Thompson Highway (Highway 11) gives access from west of Red Deer to Saskatchewan River Crossing in the northern part of Banff National Park.

Frequent public bus service to Banff townsite is operated by Greyhound Lines of Canada. The toll-free number for schedules and fares is 1-800-661-8747 (Canada and U.S.). The local number for the Banff terminal at 100 Gopher Street is (403) 762-1092. Call them regarding drop-off at Castle Junction and possibly other points along the Trans-Canada Highway (decisions are made by individual drivers based on safety and scheduling).

Brewster Transportation and Tours runs daily direct bus service from Calgary International Airport to Banff townsite. (Other companies offer frequent van service between the airport and Banff.) Brewster's toll-free number for information is 1-800-661-1152 (Canada and U.S.). Their main office at 100 Gopher St., Banff, can be reached at (403) 762-6767. The Brewster website is www.brewster.ca. The Brewster express service along the Icefields Parkway will drop off at youth hostels and trailheads on request.

At this writing, there is no public train service to Banff. Between late May and early October, however, the Great Canadian Railtour Company offers a two-day package between Vancouver and Banff with overnight in Kamloops. It's toll-free to call them at 1-800-665-7245 (Canada and U.S.).

Major car rental agencies have offices in Banff and Lake Louise. Taxi service is an option to reach trailheads.

There is an entry fee for private vehicles in national parks: the park website gives details; see Information below. Passes are available at park gates, visitor centres, and the Parks Canada office in Calgary (see below).

Information

Drop by the Parks Canada Visitor Centre at 224 Banff Avenue, Banff, to find out about park campgrounds (frontcountry and backcountry), trail conditions, wildlife warnings or closures, weather, and the park program of interpretive events.

Park staff are familiar with most areas of the park through personal experience and will give accurate and up-to-date information. They can, for example, suggest less-crowded areas, where there is a balance between impressive surroundings and solitude. This comprehensive information can be valuable, particularly before setting out on an extended backcountry trip. As Andre Dmytriev, supervisor of the Visitor Centre, put it: "It can be hard to keep to an itinerary, especially if make over-ambitious plans."

The phone number of the Banff Visitor Centre is (403) 762-1550. The fax number is (403) 762-1551.

Information on park topics—including hiking in the northern part of the park—is also available at the Parks Canada Visitor Centre in Lake Louise, phone (403) 522-3833, fax (403) 522-1212.

You can request information by e-mail to: banff_vrc@pch.gc.ca or by postal service to The Superintendent, Banff National Park, P.O. Box 900, Banff, Alberta, Canada T0L 0C0.

The Banff National Park website presents much helpful current information: www.worldweb.com/parkscanada-banff.

Parks Canada produces the *Backcountry Visitors' Guide, Banff National Park* and *Day Hikes in Banff National Park* brochures.

Information on Banff National Park is also available at the Parks Canada office of the Department of Canadian Heritage, Room 520, 220 - 4th Avenue S.E., Calgary; phone toll-free 1-800-748-7275 or local (403) 292-4401, fax (403) 292-4408. The mailing address is Suite 550, 220—4th Avenue S.E., Calgary, Alberta, Canada T2G 4X3.

Recorded information on trail conditions is available at (403) 760-1305 (Banff) and (403) 292-5478 (Calgary).

The Banff/Lake Louise Tourism Bureau can help regarding commercial accommodation and attractions in the area. It operates an information desk within the Visitor Centre at 224 Banff Avenue; phone (403) 762-8421 or write to P.O. Box 1298, Banff, Alberta, Canada T0L 0C0. Their website is www.banfflakelouise.com.

The provincial government offers a travel information service at the toll-free number 1-800-661-8888 (Canada and U.S.), or by mail from Travel Alberta, P.O. Box 2500, Edmonton, Alberta, Canada T5J 2Z1. Their website is www.travelalberta.com.

Two Visitor Information Centres under the auspices of Travel Alberta operate in the vicinity of Banff National Park: Canmore (open year-round) and Field, B.C. (seasonal). These are primarily intended as offices to visit in person; if want information by phone, please use the toll-free number above.

Accommodation

There is an extensive network of over 50 backcountry campgrounds in Banff National Park; reference to them is made throughout this book. There are also two park-operated trail shelters, at Egypt Lake and Bryant Creek. Fees apply to these facilities. For more details, contact Parks Canada as per Information above.

Parks Canada operates a network of public frontcountry campgrounds in Banff National Park. The main campground adjacent to Banff townsite is the Tunnel Mountain complex. It has over 1100 sites with varying services: 321 are fully serviced with electricity, water, and sewage; 188 are serviced with electricity only; and 618 are semi-serviced (without hook-ups). 35 sites are available for commercial groups.

There are 10 other campgrounds in the park, at locations including Two Jack Lake, Johnston Canyon, Castle Junction, Lake Louise, Mosquito Creek, and Waterfowl Lakes. Group camping is available at Two Jack Main campground. For more information, use the sources above in Information.

The Southern Alberta section of Hostelling International-Canada operates hostels in Banff townsite and Lake Louise village (the latter in affiliation with the Alpine Club of Canada). There are also generally more rustic hostels at Castle Junction, Mosquito Creek, Rampart Creek, and Hilda Creek. Reservations for all except Lake Louise can be made by phone (403) 762-4122 [in Calgary 237-8282] or via e-mail at banff@hostellingintl.ca; Lake Louise reservations can be made at (403) 522-2200 or via llouise@hostellingintl.ca. Information about these hostels is found on the website www.hostellingintl.ca/alberta.

The Alpine Club of Canada operates a network of alpine huts and shelters, as well as the Canadian Alpine Centre and International Hostel at Lake Louise (the latter in conjunction with Hostelling International-Canada). Most of the ACC's facilities are in remote locations with difficult access, though the Bow Hut near Bow Lake is not hard to reach (see p. 117). For information and reservations, call (403) 678-3200, fax (403) 678-3224, write to P.O. Box 8040, Canmore, Alberta, Canada T1W 2T8, or check their website: www.alpineclubofcanada.ca.

The three backcountry lodges in the areas of Banff National Park covered by this book are on Brewster Creek (Sundance Lodge and Halfway Lodge, phone (403) 762-4551) and the Shadow Lake Lodge (phone (403) 762-0116).

There is a wide variety of commercial accommodation in Banff National Park. Obtain information from the Banff/Lake Louise Tourism Bureau as mentioned above in Information.

Wilderness Pass and Voluntary Safety Registration

Purchase of a Wilderness Pass is mandatory for any overnight backcountry visit in Banff National Park. The Wilderness Pass specifies the backcountry campgrounds or shelters to be used, or whether in a random camping area in the remote parts of the park. A Wilderness Pass is required for bivouacing. A Wilderness Pass is included in the fee for Alpine Club of Canada huts.

An Annual Wilderness Pass is worth considering if spending seven nights or more in the backcountry over the course of a year.

Reservations can be made (for a fee) up to 90 days in advance of a backcountry trip by contacting a Parks Canada Visitor Centre (see Information above; Visitor Centres in other parks can also issue Wilderness Passes). Reservations are recommended for the peak months of July and August if set on a certain itinerary. If the Wilderness Pass is sent by mail or fax, it's suggested to stop at a Visitor Centre before setting out for updates on trail conditions, wildlife activity, closures, weather, and other pertinent information. Note that Parks Canada policy on managing human use and protecting wildlife has seen changes in backcountry access, and more changes are in the works... check before beginning a trip.

Wilderness Passes can be picked up at Visitor Centres or at the Parks Canada office in Calgary. Passes not picked up by 10 a.m. on the day of departure will be cancelled and consequent vacancies filled on a first-come, first-served basis.

If plan to engage in an activity involving significant risk, a voluntary safety registration can be made in person when purchasing or picking up the Wilderness Pass. This ensures that, if return is not made by the time indicated, a search will be initiated. A comprehensive and accurate description of the route, including any side trips, must be provided. The onus on the registrant is, of course, to report back immediately upon return: to a Visitor Centre (if open), otherwise by phone to the Banff Warden Office at (403) 762-1470 (24 hours).

Climate, Weather, and the Hiking Season

The tables below give data on the climate of Banff townsite and the Icefields Visitor Centre just north of Sunwapta Pass, two places that can be considered representative of Banff National Park. (The data for Lake Louise Village is given in *Hiking Lake Louise*.)

Each table gives the following values for the months of May through October: daily and extreme maximum and minimum temperatures, average precipitation, and average number of days with measurable precipitation.

Table 1 — Banff Townsite Climate (elevation 1397 m)

	May	June	July	Aug.	Sept.	Oct.
Daily max. (°C)	14.2	18.7	22.1	21.6	16.1	10.1
Extreme max. (°C)	29.4	33.3	34.4	33.9	31.0	26.1
Daily min. (°C)	1.5	5.4	7.4	6.8	2.7	-1.1
Extreme min. (°C)	-17.8	-3.9	-1.7	-3.3	-16.7	-27.0
Average precip. (mm)	57.5	60.0	51.2	51.3	43.8	30.3
Average days precip.	13	14	13	13	12	9

Source: *Canadian Climate Normals 1961-1990*, Environment Canada.

Table 2 — Icefields Visitor Centre Climate (elevation 1981 m)

	May	June	July	Aug.	Sept.	Oct.
Daily max. (°C)	9.1	12.1	15.2	14.3	10.3	3.5
Extreme max. (°C)	22.2	23.3	26.1	25.6	21.7	17.2
Daily min. (°C)	-3.5	0.2	2.9	2.7	-0.5	-5.9
Extreme min. (°C)	-17.8	-12.2	-9.4	-6.1	-15.0	-26.1
Average precip. (mm)	37.9	74.8	69.1	50.5	53.0	113.1
Average days precip.	11	15	13	14	14	12

Source: *Canadian Climate Normals 1951-1980*, Environment Canada.

Always keep in mind the general rule that temperature decreases and precipitation increases with an increase in elevation.

There is a recorded weather forecast for the Banff area at (403) 762-2088.

The weather (short-term conditions as compared with the long-term phenomena of climate) in Banff National Park is famous for its changeability. British climber Edward Whymper was not far off when, during a 1901 visit to the Canadian Rockies, he renamed the days of the week "Stormday, Rainday, Mistday, Hailday, Thunderday, Snowday, Sleetday." (It's not unheard of for all of these in one day!)

Be prepared for sudden changes in weather on any outdoor excursion. The high peaks on the continental divide that marks the western boundary of the park contribute to unpredictable weather. Snow can occur in any month; deep accumulations of the white stuff make travel difficult and routefinding tricky. Whiteouts also complicate navigation. Late-lying snowdrifts can remain in high mountain passes well into summer. North-facing slopes take longer to become snow-free after winter.

The hiking season in Banff National Park normally extends from May to October, varying locally with elevation and orientation. Warming temperatures and snowmelt early in the season often lead to wet and muddy conditions, unenjoyable for hiking and often resulting in damage to trails—it's best to confine spring outings to well-constructed, dry trails.

Although clear skies and reasonably mild temperatures often occur in September and October, autumn weather can be especially variable. Heavy, but usually brief, snowstorms are frequent. By late October, daytime temperatures have begun to drop, overnight lows fall below freezing, and snow may begin to pile up on the ground. These are all signs that the hiking season has drawn to a close for another year.

Looking out tent door to an overnight snowfall at Devon Lakes in late August, 1990.

Equipment

Proper equipment is essential for any outdoor activity.

On a day hike, bring clothing to keep warm and dry. Carry at least a sweater and a rain jacket; it's a good idea to also bring along rain pants and perhaps long pants if wearing shorts. A great deal of heat loss can be prevented with headgear such as a wool cap. Mitts keep hands warmer than gloves.

Layers of clothing (e.g., undershirt, shirt, sweater, jacket) allow maintenance of a comfortable temperature by adding or removing as called for. The secret is to avoid sweating, which can lead to chilling in damp clothing.

Garments of breathable material, such as polypropylene or a good Gore-tex membrane, stay drier than cotton or completely waterproof gear that can cause a soaking from the inside. Traditional wool, and new synthetics such as pile and fleece, still give some warmth when wet.

Realize that it doesn't have to be a winter blizzard for hypothermia to happen. That potentially life-threatening drop in body core temperature can occur when air temperatures are above freezing. For example, a wind speed of 30 km/hr at +4° C creates the equivalent of -8° C. Humidity, dehydration, poor nutrition, and low general fitness can also contribute to the onset of hypothermia.

Footwear should be comfortable and appropriate to the outing. Doing the *Fenland* trail in runners is fine, while a ten-day backpacking trip calls for durable boots with good ankle support. This is not to say that heavy "clodhoppers" are necessary for overnight trips...their weight means more work, and their lug sole patterns cause a surprising amount of soil erosion.

Other items to bring on a day hike include effective sunglasses, some kind of sunhat, sunscreen or sunblock (UV radiation and the risk of sunburn increase with elevation), insect repellent, first aid kit, toilet paper, an unbreakable container with water or some other drink (preferably nonalcoholic to avoid heat loss), extra food, and a knife such as one of the multi-purpose Swiss Army models.

A map is vital (see the next section); a compass can be very handy. A small flashlight or a head lamp (which has the advantage of leaving hands free) will be well worthwhile if out unexpectedly after dark. Waterproof matches or a lighter, a candle, and a survival blanket can make the difference in comfortably surviving an emergency.

Backpacking means carrying all the above, plus lots more. Rather than list all the paraphernalia, the recommendation is to get pointers. Possible sources are experienced backpackers, perhaps in a club or on a course, or books such as *Walking Softly in the Wilderness* by John Hart (Sierra Club Books, 1998). Observe what others do, and keep refining and adjusting.

Items that won't likely help much in a survival situation but that can enhance the enjoyment of an outing include camera, binoculars, hand lens, notebook, and sketchpad. There are many field guides to areas of interest such as mammals, wildflowers, birds, trees, and geology. A couple of Luminous Compositions publications fit the bill nicely (they are compact): *Central Rockies Mammals* by John Marriott and *Central Rockies Wildflowers* by Mike Potter. Another good choice is the comprehensive, entertaining *Handbook of the Canadian Rockies* by Ben Gadd (Corax Press, Jasper, Alberta, second edition 1995): this covers all the subjects mentioned and much more.

To wrap up this information on equipment, it is wise to take to heart these comments by Park Warden Tim Auger, highly-respected Public Safety Officer for Banff National Park: "The moral of the story is to be prepared to spend at least one night out before help arrives. This is only prudent, since emergency services personnel cannot always respond immediately due to factors such as poor weather or darkness. If properly equipped, a situation such as a simple sprained ankle at Cory Pass may result in a somewhat uncomfortable night out, but it won't develop into a life-threatening epic."

Map reading at the summit of Mt. Aylmer.

Topographic and Geological Maps, and Aerial Photographs

Even though most of the trails described in this book are signed, and—in conjunction with the information provided here—there should be little difficulty keeping on track, it is nevertheless imperative to have a more detailed map. This is certainly the case if venturing off-trail.

Maps are also useful for locating landmarks such as peaks, and other features including lakes, rivers, creeks, waterfalls, swamps or marshes, wooded versus open terrain, glaciers, icefields, and moraines. Cliffs and depressions are also marked, as special versions of contour lines: the thin brown lines (close together and wriggly in mountains) that represent a constant elevation. These important sources of information, derived from aerial photographs, enable determination of approximate elevation and also elevation gain or loss. The contour interval on most 1:50,000 maps is 100 feet, or 20 or 25 metres. The blue grid lines on 1:50,000 scale maps form two-centimetre squares that correspond to one square kilometre on the ground.

Precise elevations are given for such survey points as bench marks, spot elevations, control points, and surface elevations of large lakes. Topographic maps give the location of cultural (human) features, including roads, railways, bridges, buildings, and boundaries. [The latter don't always have any physical evidence.] **N.B.** Existing trails are sometimes not marked, or locations indicated are incorrect. In some instances, a

18

trail is shown where none exists. The newer the edition the more accurate, usually.

Being able to use grid references is a valuable skill: these numbers derive from the one-kilometre grid (on 1:50,000 sheets) and correspond to a location on the ground. The use of grid references is explained on the right margin of NTS 1:50,000 maps, or get other instruction. Grid references are used extensively in this book. **N.B.** Note that those given in the text are for older maps using the NAD 27 system; newer maps using the NAD 83 system have slightly different grid references for the same location.

As mentioned in Using This Guidebook (p. 11), there are two good choices of maps for hiking: the Gem Trek series and the government NTS series. Both (where available) are mentioned in the trail descriptions. Each NTS map has a name from an important feature (e.g., Hector Lake) and a code (e.g., 82 N/9).

A 1:200,000 scale map of Banff, Kootenay, and Yoho national parks is available. This map, in which each five-centimetre square represents 100 square kilometres on the ground, does not give sufficient detail to be suitable for hiking but can be of use to give a general overview of the area and to identify faraway peaks.

Maps are sold by the Friends of Banff National Park at their outlets in the two Parks Canada Visitors Centres. This not-for-profit cooperating association supports many projects in the park; a catalogue can be requested at phone (403) 762-8918, fax (403) 762-2933, or by mail from P.O. Box 2590, Banff, Alberta, Canada T0L 0C0. Their website is www.canadianrockies.net/friendsofbanff/

Maps are also sold at other locations including The Viewpoint, Book & Art Den, Monod Sports, and Mountain Magic Equipment in Banff, Woodruff & Blum Booksellers in Lake Louise, and the Alpine Club of Canada national office in Canmore. In Calgary, Mountain Equipment Co-op, Map Town, and Mapworld are among the choices.

A series of geological maps at 1:50,000 scale published by the Geological Survey of Canada gives fascinating information on the complex, intriguing geological formations of some areas of Banff National Park. (Complimentary "structure sections" showing cross-sections of the mountains accompany the maps.) Contact the GSC Bookstore, 3303 - 33rd St. N.W., Calgary, Alberta, Canada T2L 2A7; phone (403) 292-7030.

Aerial photographs, as well as single-frame Landsat prints, slides, and satellite photomosaics, are available from the National Air Photo Library, 615 Booth Street, Ottawa, Ontario, Canada K1A 0E9; phone toll-free 1-800-230-6275.

Safety

The activities described in this guidebook are not inherently dangerous but do hold an element of risk. To be safe, always practise common sense and be aware of potential pitfalls and act accordingly. As stated in the *Backcountry Visitors' Guide* produced by Banff National Park: "Your safety is your personal responsibility. Caution and self-reliance are essential. You or your trip leader should have a knowledge of natural hazards, experience in avoiding them, and a plan to deal with them successfully when required."

The best approach is to be as well informed as possible before heading out, and to choose trips based on personal capabilities and experience. Andre Dmytriev, supervisor of the Banff Visitor Centre, suggests trying a shakedown trip first if new to (or rusty at) an activity. As he puts it: "Pushing to the limit reduces your enjoyment and can lead to problems."

In addition to points mentioned above (such as using proper equipment, being prepared for weather changes, having a good map, and possibly taking out a voluntary safety registration), following is information on several topics of particular relevance to safety.

Bear warning sign.

Bears—Both black bears and grizzly bears occur in Banff National Park. Bears are naturally wary of humans and generally choose to avoid them. However, bears may threaten and even attack people when accustomed to humans, when surprised, or when defending themselves, their young, or food.

Park visitor centres and warden offices have information on bear sightings and on areas that have been posted with bear warnings or area closures due to bear activity.

Below follows some background, though because of the many possible factors involved, it's difficult to give succinct information on how to avoid bears and how to act in the rare situation of an encounter with a bear. Bears are very intelligent and complex animals; each bear and any encounter is unique. There is no single strategy that will work in all situations.

For more detailed information, read the excellent book *Bear Attacks: Their Causes and Avoidance* by Dr. Stephen Herrero. It gives much practical information on bear biology and on precautions and actions to take in a multitude of situations. Dr. Herrero, a professor at the University of Calgary, is an internationally recognized authority on bears who has done extensive field work in Banff National Park.

The Parks Canada brochure *Keep the Wild in Wildlife* has information on how to reduce the risk of bear encounters. If not received when entering the park, this brochure is available at park frontcountry campgrounds and at visitor centres.

Interpretive programs can give good information on bears.

An important step is to know how to distinguish between a black bear and a grizzly bear. The most noticeable identifying characteristics of a grizzly bear are the prominent hump at the shoulders and the long, gradually curved claws, neither of which are present in black bears. Colour is not a reliable way to tell the two species apart: black bears can be black or brown, while grizzly bears can be black, blond, or a "silver-tipped" brown.

In general, the best thing to do when travelling in bear country is to take preventive measures. Learn to recognize sign (tracks, scat, diggings, torn-up logs, overturned rocks) and likely habitat (e.g., berry patches, avalanche paths), and change plans if warranted. Clear out if happen upon a dead animal; a concentration of ravens can be a sign of a kill. {Report this to Parks Canada.}

It is safer to travel in a group of at least three. Keep children within reach. Travel during daylight hours, and stick to established trails where possible.

Make lots of noise {clap, call out, sing, talk loudly, whatever} while hiking, especially in places where it would be hard to be seen, heard, or smelled by a bear, e.g., among dense vegetation, near a rushing stream, or if there is a headwind. The idea here is to alert any bear, for once aware it will most often leave the area—possibly without even having signalled its presence. Note that bear bells, though popular, are not much use in situations such as high wind or rushing water that drown out their sound.

When camping (both frontcountry and backcountry), keep a fastidiously clean campsite. Cook downwind well away—at least 100 metres—from sleeping quarters. Wash and store all dishes and utensils immediately after use. Strain food particles from dishwater and store with garbage. Dump dishwater in designated sumps, or at least 100 metres from sleeping areas. Do not burn or bury garbage: pack it out in airtight containers and handle it the same way as food.

Keep sleeping bags and tents completely free of food, beverages, and associated odours. Don't sleep in clothes worn while cooking.

Overnight or while away from a tent, store away food and anything else with a strong odour (e.g., food scraps, garbage, cooking pots, stove, dirty dishcloths, and toiletries such as toothpaste, soap, and deodorant if used). Storage should be either up the bear-proof systems provided at designated backcountry campgrounds, or up a personally rigged system when in a random camping zone. The latter option requires rope so that the stuff is suspended at least four metres off the ground and two metres from any tree trunk. Proper storage will also prevent raids by small animals.

If a bear is seen in the distance, observe it. Wait to see whether it moves away. If so, advance cautiously. Back away and move off slowly if the bear stays on the trail ahead or if it comes closer. Leave the area, or perhaps take a detour to proceed. Always leave a bear an escape route.

Never run away from a bear. Bears can run as fast as a racehorse, both uphill and downhill.

Stay calm in a bear situation. Keep together if in a group and immediately pick up any small children. Back away slowly, perhaps speaking calmly and firmly to establish yourself as a human and not a prey animal. A scream or sudden movement may trigger an attack. Avoid direct eye contact, which a bear could perceive as threatening. A pack can provide protection in case of an attack, although shedding a pack can assist in climbing if there is a suitable tree to escape a grizzly bear (see below) and the dropped pack could serve as a distraction.

Climbing a tree may be a possible escape, though black bears climb readily and subadult grizzlies can do so (contrary to widespread belief). Adult grizzly bears can sometimes get up a short distance, and can reach up as high as three metres (10 ft) without taking their hind feet off the ground. The minimum recommended safe height is 10 metres (33 ft).

Black bears are agile tree climbers, using the short, curved claws that may have evolved to allow them to escape grizzly bears, their worst natural enemies. However, although incidents have been recorded in which a black bear pursued an attack upon a person up a tree, this is not the norm.

If there is no suitable tree, a cliff or a lake may offer an avenue of escape (though bears do swim).

Most bears don't attack; they usually try to avoid humans or ensure that they don't represent a threat. A bear may rear up on its hind legs and wave its nose about in an attempt at identification. A bear may make a bluff charge in which it veers away at close quarters.

If contact is imminent, use bear spray if at hand. Do realize that the effectiveness of bear spray is not guaranteed. For a start, it has to be readily available, preferably in an easily reached holster. Recent research indicates that bear spray can be effective against some bears when used properly. However, wind, spray distance, rain, and product shelf life can all affect how well it works. Carefully read directions beforehand, and don't allow possession of bear spray to let cockiness prevail.

If contact occurs, play dead. Lie face down with legs spread to prevent being rolled over. Protect face, neck, and back of the head with arms and hands. Remain still until the bear leaves the area. Fighting usually increases the intensity of an attack, although in some cases it has caused the bear to leave. An attack seldom last more than a few minutes; if it persists for more than several minutes, consider fighting.

However, if a bear stalks and attacks, or attacks at night, do **not** play dead. In this case, try to escape, possibly up a tree. Use spray, shout, wave a branch, throw rocks...do whatever it takes to let the bear know it isn't looking at easy prey. This kind of attack is rare but can be very serious since it often means that the bear is looking for food and might even consider a human as prey.

Bears are integral and important members of the ecological communities of national parks and wilderness areas. Although they should be accorded a healthy respect as powerful and unpredictable wild creatures, they should not be feared. Knowledge will give an understanding and appreciation of these animals, allowing enjoyment of appropriate activities.

With correct practises, it's unlikely a bear will even be seen on a trail or in the backcountry. Ironically, the best chance of sighting a bear may be along park roads. (There too proper steps must be followed for mutual safety.)

Other animals—Cougars live in Banff National Park. Although not often seen because of their usually solitary, elusive nature and nocturnal preferences, there is the possibility of an encounter with one. Cougars may be more active in areas like towns and campgrounds that have habituated prey. The best measures, as with bears, are preventive, so make noise and travel in a group if possible. Keep children close at hand, and immediately pick up a small child if a cougar is sighted. With a cougar, do **not** play dead and do not run. Face the animal and retreat slowly, increasing apparent size by raising arms or an object overhead. Be aggressive to deter an attack: shout, wave a stick, throw stones.

To date other large carnivores such as wolves and wolverines have not represented a safety hazard to hikers or backpackers in Banff National Park.

Coyotes have inflicted minor injuries to young people and to people sleeping out in the open; these incidents have usually occurred in areas where coyotes have become habituated to humans (such as near townsites or campgrounds).

Elk are dangerous, especially during calving season (mid-May to the end of June) when cow elk are protective of their young, and during mating season (mid-September to the end of October) when bull elk are aggressive. Parks Canada recommends staying at least 30 metres (100 ft) away from elk at all times—this distance is equal to three bus lengths.

Moose are even bigger than elk, and if sighted should also be given a wide berth.

Ground squirrels can inflict a sharp bite, so abide by park regulations prohibiting feeding or enticing them.

Ticks—The Rocky Mountain wood tick is a small (about 5 mm or 1/4 inch long), mostly reddish-brown, flat-bodied, eight-legged arachnid: of the same class as spiders but in a different order. Ticks, which need mammal blood as part of their life cycle, are often abundant on animals such as elk, moose, and bighorn sheep, to which they usually do little harm.

However, ticks will also attempt to use humans as hosts, and can induce paralysis or transmit potentially fatal Rocky Mountain spotted fever.

Ticks are most active in Banff National Park from April to June. They occur most often on dry, grassy slopes—especially those frequented by ground squirrels—up to about 2100 metres (almost 7000 ft) elevation. As preventive measures against ticks, wear long pants tucked into socks and don't sit or stretch out in areas likely to harbour ticks. An insect repellent containing DEET can be applied to clothing that will come into contact with grasses or low shrubs. Ticks do not drop from trees.

After any outing, check thoroughly—and help any companions check—for ticks that may have hitched a ride. Look especially carefully around the head and neck, in other hairy areas, and where clothing is constricted. Ticks usually spend at least three hours looking for a place to draw off blood, generally climbing up in their search, so there is a good chance of brushing them off before they inflict any damage. (Ticks do not sting.) If at home or in a place where a tick might return for another try, it should be flushed down the toilet or crushed with footwear or a solid object (**not** fingers); this isn't necessary on a hike.

If a tick has become attached and begun feeding (which it does by painlessly inserting its mouthparts through the skin), the best procedure is to remove the whole body by pulling steadily but gently. Grasp it near the head to try to get the mouthparts out. Don't try such folk remedies as burning the tick's rear or dousing it with alcohol: this will only kill it while still embedded. If the mouthparts stay in, remove them by teasing out with a heated needle or knife. Then wash the wound thoroughly with soap and sterilize it with antiseptic if possible.

If a tick has fed, the person should see a doctor. If it has remained unnoticed for several days, signs of tick paralysis may develop: numbness in the extremities, loss of coordination, and drowsiness. These conditions clear up within a few hours once the tick is removed.

In the rare case of infection with potentially fatal Rocky Mountain spotted fever, a high temperature will ensue and severe headache, chills, muscle pain, and a cough. Later a rash usually covers the arms and legs, and sometimes other parts of the body. Get immediate treatment if any of these symptoms appear.

To alleviate concerns (without of course dismissing the future possibility), it may be a relief to learn that there have been no cases of tick paralysis or Rocky Mountain spotted fever reported from Banff National Park in over 15 years.

At time of writing, there have been no confirmed cases of Lyme disease traceable to Alberta, but it may appear soon. It is usually transmitted by tiny (pinhead-sized) deer ticks, which are now present but so far do not carry the disease.

Hantavirus—Droppings and urine from mice can contain potentially deadly hantavirus. Infection initially causes flu-like symptoms, with shortness of breath and increased heart rate later developing. Over 60 percent of untreated cases result in death from lungs filled with fluid.

Store food as securely as possible, and wear rubber gloves and a respirator if cleaning up after mice in places such as a trail shelter or an alpine hut.

Water—Drinking water is a safety concern in the backcountry due to the possibility of giardiasis, the ailment commonly known as "beaver fever." Despite their pristine appearance, the streams, rivers, and lakes of Banff National Park can harbour the protozoan parasite *Giardia lamblia*.

The symptoms of *Giardia* infection do not appear until 10 to 15 days after contamination. They include diarrhoea, stomach cramps, poor appetite, and general lethargy. If these signs appear and giardiasis is suspected, see a doctor.

As always, the best approach is to take preventive measures. To avoid this illness, use an appropriate portable filter or boil for at least five minutes all water for drinking, cooking, and personal hygiene. Practise good sanitation, including using outhouses where available. If there is no loo, defecate at least 100 metres away from any water source, digging a small hole 15-20 cm deep and covering it afterward. The title may sound flippant, but an entire book has been written on the subject of proper outdoor human waste disposal practises: *How to Shit in the Woods* (Kathleen Meyer, Ten Speed Press, 1989).

Be careful to avoid dehydration.

Fording the stream below Bow Glacier Falls.

Fords—In a different context from drinking, water can present another hazard: that of crossing streams and rivers on foot. Fords can be a tricky business: drowning due to a slip while trying to negotiate a high, swift-flowing, numbingly cold mountain torrent is a distinct possibility. Many of the backcountry trails in Banff National Park that entail fords are best left for late summer when the season's heaviest snowmelt is over. Also be aware that sudden rainfall or high temperatures causing increased glacial melt can also make fords difficult.

Prepare for any such crossing by finding a pole (or using an ice axe or solid walking pole) to serve as a third point of contact and to provide support. The recommendation is to plant the brace upstream and face into the current while crossing. If in a group, link arms and/or wrap them around a pole held horizontally.

It's a good idea to carry lightweight runners or sports sandals: they are nice to change into at the end of a day of backpacking, plus can serve for crossings. They give better purchase than bare feet, particularly on slippery rocks or in cold water. If those conditions prevail and there is no alternative, crossing in boots is wise. Put on dry spare socks afterward, and hopefully dry out the footwear overnight if on a backpacking trip (e.g., at the campfire if permitted).

Before heading across a ford, make sure everything is secure—the exception being a backpack waistbelt, which should be left undone so that it can be dumped quickly if get into trouble. If the current becomes too strong or too high in the course of an attempted crossing, retreat and look for a wider (thus usually shallower) place to ford. Or wait for the water level to drop, as it will after a sudden rainstorm has passed or by early morning on a glacially fed watercourse if there have been warm midday temperatures.

If a ford is not feasible, discretion is the better part of valour: back off and perhaps choose another route.

Lightning—This powerful natural phenomenon poses significant danger to outdoor enthusiasts. Its frequency is attested to by the fact that around the globe there are up to 100 lightning strikes per second.

Warning signs that lightning may be about to strike in the immediate vicinity include a sensation of itchy skin, hair moving and standing out, and crackling sounds from metal objects such as an ice axe or fishing rod.

The chances of being hit by the main path of a lightning bolt, which is often deadly, are remote. Many people struck by secondary paths—not as powerful as the main path but still packing a wallop—do survive.

The main danger from being hit by lightning is cardiac arrest. The strike can short-circuit the heart's electrical system, and the heart may not spontaneously restart. Anyone who is conscious immediately after being hit by lightning will almost certainly recover, but a lightning strike victim who is unconscious is probably in cardiac arrest and requires immediate CPR (cardiopulmonary resuscitation) and medical attention.

The following suggestions will not guarantee avoiding lightning (like many natural forces, it is unpredictable), but they will improve the odds against being hit:

— Never take shelter under an isolated tree: this mistake claims the single largest group of lightning fatalities. If lightning strikes the tree, a secondary discharge or ground current could hit anyone beneath. In addition, lightning can cause instant vaporization of the sap, exploding the tree.

— During a thunderstorm, don't become the tallest object by standing in an open area. If have to stay in the open, look for a depression in which to crouch down. Keep feet together to minimize the danger from ground current.

— If on a ridge, head down.

— Move away from open water since people are often the highest object in such an area.

— Set aside any metal objects, such as an ice axe or fishing rod. These do not attract lightning but can result in burns.

Off-trail travel—Travel beyond established trails, such as on any of the scrambles described in this book, requires awareness of such natural hazards as cliffs and canyons, and unstable scree, talus, and moraines. Other dangers include rockfall, cornices (windblown deposits of snow hanging out from a ridge over nothing but air—don't venture near their edges), and avalanches (yes, even in spring and summer; spontaneous cornice collapse due to weakening in warm temperatures is one cause).

Cornice at summit of Mt. Bourgeau, with section about to avalanche.

An ice axe is necessary to travel on steep snow, and of course it should be more than just decoration...knowledge of how to self-arrest is what it's for. Take a course or get pointers from someone else who knows. Avoid icy gullies or slopes that may have ice under a thin layer of snow.

The scope of this guidebook does not include glacier travel, which calls for specialized equipment and knowledge of specific hazards including crevasses, moulins (millwells), and glacier caves.

Interpretive Events

Parks Canada staff offer a slate of events that can give insights into the natural and human heritage of Banff National Park. These include guided walks and hikes, evening programs, films, roving exhibits, and special events. Some of these are free (sometimes with limited space), others have a charge. A schedule of regular events is given in *The Mountain Guide* newsletter. Visitor centres and frontcountry campgrounds also have this information.

Parks Canada interpreter Heather Dempsey leading a guided hike.

Interpretive events are also presented by a number of private businesses, including Willow Root Nature Tours, P.O. Box 995, Banff, Alberta, Canada T0L 0C0; phone (403) 762-4335; and White Mountain Adventures, #7 - 107 Boulder Crescent, Canmore, Alberta, Canada T1W 1K9; phone toll-free 1-800-408-0005 or (403) 678-4099.

Other Pursuits

In addition to the activities described in this book, there are many other self-propelled pursuits to enjoy in Banff National Park. These include mountain biking (subject to restrictions), bicycle touring, rockclimbing, mountaineering, canoeing, kayaking, and winter activities such as cross-country skiing and snowshoeing.

Abundant information on these topics is available at visitor centres and in other publications.

Some Relevant National Park Regulations

In additions to the requirements mentioned above, such as the mandatory Wilderness Pass for overnight trips, there are other rules to follow while in Banff National Park: these are for everyone's benefit, including the wildlife.

— Within the backcountry, zoning (e.g., Outdoor Recreation, Natural Environment, Wilderness, and Special Preservation) governs overnight camping. Designated backcountry campgrounds must be used in the zones where they are provided. Random camping is permitted in certain areas under specified conditions. For details, contact a visitor centre or consult the *Backcountry Visitors' Guide* brochure.

— Fires are only permitted at certain backcountry campgrounds, where the metal fireboxes provided must be used. If choose to have a fire, keep it small and use only deadfall. Tend a fire at all times and douse it completely before leaving. In random camping areas, any traces of fire must be removed, inluding fire rings. Lightweight backpacking stoves are recommended for cooking as they are clean and efficient; they are obligatory if there is a fire ban or if at a backcountry campground where fires are prohibited.

— Dogs must be restrained on a leash at all times in a national park. Pets may provoke a confrontation with wildlife such as bears or cougars; they can also attract wood ticks. It might be better to leave pets at home.

— Feeding, enticing, touching, or harassing wildlife are prohibited; conviction can result in a substantial fine. Feeding an animal interferes with its natural foraging and can cause habituation, in which the animal loses its natural wariness around humans. This can affect its survival and lead to injury to people. Most people are well aware of the illegality of feeding wildlife, particularly bears; it applies equally to smaller creatures such as ground squirrels and gray jays.

— Leave all wildflowers, plants, trees, rocks, fossils, horns, antlers, nests, eggs, and any other natural or historical objects undisturbed—for others to enjoy and since that is where they belong.

— The "pack-in, pack-out" policy is in force in national parks: do not leave behind any garbage on an outing. Do not bury food scraps, which can easily be discovered and dug up by wildlife. If you dispose of garbage in a fire (where permitted), burn only combustible matter and ensure that it is completely consumed. Anything not quickly biodegradable should be packed out. A free litter bag is issued with the Wilderness Pass required for overnight trips. Good planning will keep the amount of garbage generated on a trip to a minimum. Good stewardship suggests taking out any garbage left by others, to leave an area better than found.

— A valid national parks fishing licence is required to go angling within a national park. Licences can be purchased at visitor centres, the Parks Canada office in Calgary (see p. 13), and other locations such as Home Hardware and Monod's Sports in Banff.

— The use of firearms in national parks is illegal. Any firearms in transport must be kept sealed and unloaded, with ammunition stored separately. Firearms cannot be taken onto any trail or into the backcountry. A Wildlife Watch program is in effect in Banff National Park. Call 911 in Banff National Park to immediately report suspicious activity or a poaching incident (or any violation of park regulations). [Other options are to call toll-free 1-888-WARDENS (927-3367) or (403) 762-1470 in the Banff area.] If witness to an infraction, observe from a distance and get as many details as possible but don't endanger personal safety.

Some Final Suggestions

Here are some pointers that may be helpful:

— It's generally recommended not to travel alone in the outdoors, for reasons of safety. Sharing observations and experiences can enhance an outing.

— When on established trails, keep to the path. Avoid shortcutting, which is hard on the environment and ultimately harder on the body. Shortcuts, especially on switchbacks, cause erosion and lead to maintenance problems. So does the unnecessary creation of new trails: wear appropriate footwear and think about impact. Even if there are muddy sections, stay on the beaten path. Prevent unsightly and destructive trail braiding.

— If in a group travelling off-trail, disperse rather than concentrate, i.e., spread out rather than going single file. Choose a route to avoid trampling vegetation as much as possible by passing over rock or bare ground.

— When backpacking, use a tent with a waterproof floor and a rainfly. Refrain from trenching, and definitely do not follow the archaic practice of making a bough bed (cutting live branches to sleep on). That idea belongs to the Dark Ages. Instead take an inflatable sleeping pad (e.g., Therm-a-Rest) or a closed cell foam pad.

— Do any washing—of dishes, of clothes, personal hygiene—well away from water sources (at least 100 metres). Pour any dirty or soapy water into a waste sump or at least a shallow hole that is covered over; don't introduce it directly into water sources. Ditto for toothpaste.

— Do not tempt a porcupine attracted to salt by leaving around gear such as boots and backpacks with leather attachment points. Also, close and latch outhouse doors upon leaving; otherwise, a porcupine could damage the interior.

— Don't take cans or bottles on backpacking trips, because of weight, possibility of breakage, and garbage concerns. If necessary, repackage food into required quantities. Pouch-packed and freeze-dried foods are usually lightweight, tasty, and resonably priced. Pick a menu that requires the least possible amount of cooking, thus conserving fuel as well as saving time. Choose food that does not give off strong, animal-attracting odours (fish and meat have drawbacks in this regard). Try to gauge quantities so that all of a meal will be eaten; this reduces leftovers or garbage. If possible, cook meals for which clean-up is easy.

— Be environmentally responsible with respect to outdoor activities (seems obvious, doesn't it?). Practise the credo of "reduce, re-use, recycle." Take advantage of recycling facilities (such as in Banff, Lake Louise, and Canmore) for such materials as paper, newsprint, cardboard, tin, glass, and redeemable beverage containers. If in a private vehicle, observe the speed limit. Speeding wastes gasoline and endangers wildlife and people (including speeders); besides, a big reason for getting outdoors is usually to relax! Another conservation measure is to take into account the amount of driving for a given hike: does it make sense to drive for hours for a 20 minute walk? Several short outings could be combined over a couple of days or so.

Overall, the slogan "Be prepared." holds true. Observing this simple advice often makes the difference between a rewarding outing and a disappointing one.

As pioneer explorer and climber Walter Wilcox wrote in *Camping in the Canadian Rockies* (1896): "Mountain adventures (...) comprise all the scale of sensations, from those marked by the pains of extreme exhaustion, physical weakness, hunger, and cold, to those of the greatest exhilaration and pleasure. Fortunately, the sensations of pleasure are by far the more abundant."

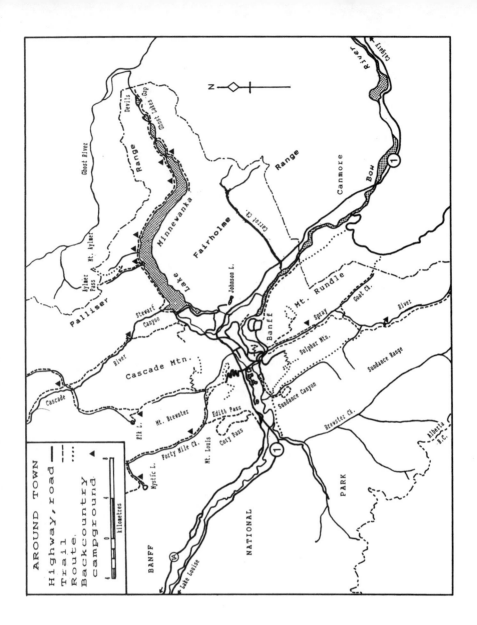

AROUND TOWN

Highway, road ———
Trail ....
Route. ....
Backcountry
campground ▲

30

Around Town

East face of Cascade Mountain from near end of *Lower Cascade Valley* trail.

Tunnel Mountain

Distance: 2.3 km (1.4 mi) — St. Julien Road to summit of Tunnel Mountain
Day hike: 30 minutes—1 hour one way
Elevation gain: 240 m (790 ft)
Maximum elevation: 1690 m (5545 ft)
Maps: Gem Trek 1:35,000 Banff Up-Close and NTS 1:50,000 Banff 82-O/4
Trailhead: Banff Centre overflow parking area in Banff townsite, on the east side of St. Julien Road, 350 metres south of its intersection with the east end of Wolf Street. An alternate trailhead is at km 0.3 of this trail, where it crosses Tunnel Mountain Drive 500 metres north of the east end of St. Julien Road.

0.0 — Sign with hiker symbol (elevation 1450 m) at northwest corner of parking area. Climb, steeply at first, then on more gradual switchbacks.
0.3 — Cross Tunnel Mountain Drive (1495 m); continue climbing on well-graded switchbacks.
1.9 — Reach summit ridge; turn north and continue climbing.
2.3 — Summit of Tunnel Mountain (1690 m).

Looking west up the Bow Valley from summit of Tunnel Mountain, over Banff townsite to the Massive Range.

Northeast face of Mt. Rundle from Tunnel Mountain.

The well-designed switchbacks up the west side of Tunnel Mountain give a relatively easy opportunity to reach the top of a Rockies peak. Granted it is a low one, yet reaching the summit reveals sweeping views up and down the Bow Valley. As explorer Walter Wilcox wrote in 1896, it is "the best place from which to get a good general idea of the topography of Banff and its surroundings."

Starting from within Banff townsite, the trail climbs through a forest with much lodgepole pine, recognized by tight egg-shaped cones and needles growing in pairs. There is also lots of Douglas-fir, with furrowed bark and the cones' mousetail-like bracts. In the more open terrain at the summit ridge is found limber pine, featuring large cones and needles in clusters of five.

As gain elevation, the vistas to the west over the townsite and toward the Vermilion Lakes and Mt. Bourgeau become more expansive. At km 1.9, where the trail turns sharply north, is the first look east down the Bow Valley from the edge of the precipitous eastern cliffs of Tunnel Mountain. (A safety fence was installed in 1998.)

The shape of Tunnel Mountain resulted from its complete submergence during glaciation. The ice glided up the west side of this bedrock knob, but on the east side carried off rock loosened by repeated freezing and thawing of water in crevices. The rounded appearance of Tunnel Mountain contrasts markedly with the sharp summits of nearby, higher peaks such as Mt. Rundle and Cascade Mountain, whose crests were not smoothed by glaciers.

Despite its name, there is no tunnel in Tunnel Mountain. There were plans to build one in the 1880s, courtesy of the at-times impetuous Major A.B. Rogers. In laying out the line for the westward-progressing Canadian Pacific Railway, he proposed to run right through the peak. The obstacle was to be breached by blasting a tunnel.

However, a less expensive route in the valley to the north was settled upon following a re-evaluation by surveyor Charles Shaw, who wrote: "Rogers' location here was the most extraordinary blunder I have ever known in the way of engineering." Thus dynamite was never used to bore through the mountain, but the name given in anticipation by the CPR has stuck.

There has been consideration given to applying the translation of the Native name, "Sleeping Bison," whose aptness is evident in several views.

Bow River Hoodoos

Distance: 0.5 km (0.3 mi) — Tunnel Mountain Road to point above hoodoos
Walk: 10 minutes one way
Elevation gain: 5 m (16 ft)
Maximum elevation: 1410 m (4625 ft)
Maps: Gem Trek 1:35,000 Banff Up-Close and NTS 1:50,000 Banff 82-O/4
Trailhead: Hoodoos viewpoint parking area on south side of Tunnel Mountain Road, 2.1 km (1.3 mi) east of its junction with Tunnel Mountain Drive. The parking area is across from Tunnel Mountain campground, between the entrances for the hook-up and no hook-up sections.

   0.0 — South side of parking area (elevation 1405 m). Follow path, paved at first, to and beyond interpretive signs.
   0.5 — Point on established trail (1410 m) directly above hoodoos.

Bow River Hoodoos.

Red osier dog-wood berries.

The Bow River Hoodoos are distinctively shaped pillars located on an open slope above the river near Tunnel Mountain campground. A short stroll leads to a point above these mysterious minarets, spiritually significant to Native people.

Hoodoos—a generic term for such columns of earth—are puzzling for geomorphologists (scientists studying the formation of landscape features) because they can result from various processes and take on different appearances. The Bow River Hoodoos seem to have originated from a jumbled deposit of mud and stones, cemented by a precipitate of calcium carbonate (lime). This deposit was acted upon by rain and snowmelt; the caprocks that protected the soft material beneath from being washed away have since fallen.

Near the start of the trail leading above the hoodoos grows Rocky Mountain juniper, a small, bushy tree (here rarely more than four metres high). It is near the northern limit of its range on these dry south-facing slopes. This is in the same genus as the abundant shrubs creeping juniper and common juniper that are also found here, but this rare evergreen has a less prostrate growth form. Limber pine (*Pinus flexilis*) is common in this area.

It's a steep scramble from the end of this trail down to the base of the hoodoos to take a closer look; if do so, be careful not to cause additional erosion.

A former roadway continues along the terrace for a kilometre or so, allowing a longer amble if so inclined. This extension leads closer to the prominent east face of Mt. Rundle, with its well-defined sedimentary strata. Wandering this way also gives a good view of the eastern aspect of Tunnel Mountain; this is one of the views that makes clear the derivation of the Native name meaning "Sleeping Bison." The old road eventually narrows to a footpath, turns into the trees, and ultimately dead-ends at the Cascade River.

An alternative trail to or from the Bow River Hoodoos links this trailhead with Tunnel Mountain Drive at the sharp bend above Bow Falls. From this trailhead, the 4.7 km (2.9 mi) connector runs west parallel to Tunnel Mountain Road before angling down toward the Bow River. The meadows by the river often harbour elk. The trail then skirts the south cliffs of Tunnel Mountain before climbing to the Bow Falls viewpoint, from which connection can be made to the *Bow River* trail.

Fenland

Distance: 2.1 km (1.3 mi) — Loop that can be started at several points
Walk: 20—30 minute loop
Elevation gain: Negligible
Maximum elevation: 1380 m (4530 ft)
Maps: Gem Trek 1:35,000 Banff Up-Close and NTS 1:50,000 Banff 82-O/4
Trailhead: The main trailhead is at the Forty Mile Creek picnic area, on the west side of Mt. Norquay Road 400 metres north of the railroad crossing. Other trail-heads are on the west side of Mt. Norquay Road 25 metres north of the railroad crossing and again just south of the bridge over Forty Mile Creek, and on the south side of Vermilion Lakes Drive 600 metres from its start off Mt. Norquay Rd.

0.0 — Forty Mile Creek picnic area (elevation 1380 m). Cross footbridge and keep straight.
0.3 — Keep right; left leads to Mt. Norquay Road in 100 metres.
1.7 — Keep straight; trail to left over footbridge leads to Vermilion Lakes Drive.
2.1 — Cross footbridge back to picnic area (1380 m).

Bull elk scratching itself with antler.

Canada goose.

The *Fenland* trail gives insights into intriguing ecology. Among the various types of wetland, a fen is drier than a marsh but wetter than a bog or a swamp. The biologically productive mosaic of water, grasses, sedges, and shrubs found in a fen represents ideal habitat for creatures such as elk, beaver, and voles. (The latter are small rodents that look like mice but have distinct characteristics.)

Along this trail there are areas in transition to swamp, the driest wetland (if that isn't an oxymoron), featuring white spruce trees, shrubs, mosses, and a spongy floor.

Birdwatching along the *Fenland* trail is rewarding. Such species as Canada goose, mallard, hairy woodpecker, black-capped chickadee, and yellow-rumped warbler can usually be sighted. If fortunate, a barred owl or a kingfisher might be seen, or at least heard.

The belted kingfisher, to give the full name of the species found here, is so-called because of bands of colour on the breast: blue on white in the male, blue and rust on white in the female. These fascinating birds, whose crests make their heads appear disproportionately large, are often first noticed by their loud rattling call.

Kingfishers dive head-first for fish from a perch over water, or from the air (sometimes hovering briefly over potential prey). Their nests are long burrows dug using their heavy bills and stubby feet. A belted kingfisher is pictured on the current (2001) Canadian $5 bill, though the design may soon change.

Cyclists often use this trail, so be ready to step aside quickly since they have limited visibility due to the twists and turns.

Vermilion Lakes

Distance: 4.3 km (2.7 mi) — Mt. Norquay Road to end of Vermilion Lakes Drive
Walk: 1—1.5 hour(s) one way
Elevation loss: 10 m (33 ft)
Elevation gain: 5 m (16 ft)
Maximum elevation: 1385 m (4540 ft)
Maps: Gem Trek 1:35,000 Banff Up-Close and NTS 1:50,000 Banff 82-O/4
Trailhead: Junction of Vermilion Lakes Drive with Mt. Norquay Road 700 metres north of railroad crossing.

0.0 — Intersection (elevation 1385 m). Follow paved road—watch for traffic.
0.6 — Unmarked junction with short path to south leading to footbridge over Forty Mile Creek and so to the *Fenland* trail.
0.9 — Pulloff to south for First Vermilion Lake.
1.9 — Pulloff to south for Second Vermilion Lake.
3.7 — Parking area and restrooms to south.
3.9 — Pulloff to south for Third Vermilion Lake.
4.3 — End of Vermilion Lakes Drive (1380 m) and turnaround area.

Walking along Vermilion Lakes Drive just outside Banff townsite hardly constitutes a wilderness experience, what with the traffic on it and the dull roar from that on the nearby Trans-Canada Highway. However, filtering out the noise and watching for vehicles make going on foot along this dead-end road amply rewarding.

Elk, mule deer, and coyote are often observed along the chain of three shallow lakes. Other species that might be seen include muskrat, beaver, mink, black bear, moose, and (rarely in summer) wolf.

Mt. Rundle (right) and Tunnel Mountain (centre) reflected in First Vermilion Lake.

Osprey at Vermilion Lakes nest.

The birdlife is phenomenal at the Vermilion Lakes, ranging from tiny hummingbirds to large raptors (birds that capture prey with their talons).

Osprey and bald eagle are two examples of raptors, and both nest here. There is excellent opportunity to witness these two species, which have magnificent wingspans. Both are making a comeback from the ravages of DDT, although ospreys and many other migratory birds are still exposed to the insidious pesticide on their wintering grounds. A smaller raptor, the American kestrel, is fairly common, and eyecatching with its reddish plumage.

Water birds are abundant. Canada geese nest at the lakes, as do red-necked grebes at Third Vermilion Lake. Other species of grebes may be seen. Common loons with their large, dark profile are often spotted, and their ethereal calls heard. Binoculars or a spotting scope can bring out their intricate black-and-white pattern.

Tundra swans are seen in small numbers during spring and fall migration. Ducks to expect include the ubiquitous mallard, as well as green-winged teal, Barrow's goldeneye, and the fish-eating common merganser. Shorebirds to look for are killdeer, greater yellowlegs, and the tail-bobbing spotted sandpiper. A common snipe is usually identified by the fluttering "woo-woo-woo" sound made by wind over its tail feathers in display flight—ventriloquistic it is, since even after hearing the bird it can be difficult to pick out swooping high overhead.

A wide variety of songbirds can be sighted at the Vermilion Lakes, including flycatchers, swallows, warblers, and sparrows. Among the regular species are red-winged blackbird (the males of which are well known for their flashy epaulets), ruby-crowned kinglet, common yellowthroat, and eastern kingbird.

A fascinating aspect of the story of the Vermilion Lakes is archaeological evidence indicating human activity here some 11,500 years ago. Thus we know that Native people occupied the area, at least on a seasonal basis, over one hundred centuries ago...kind of makes our documented history, at about twenty decades, seem pretty short, doesn't it?

Cave & Basin Marsh

Distance: 1.5 km (0.9 mi) — Cave & Basin parking area to *Sundance Canyon* trail
Walk: 20—30 minutes one way
Elevation gain: Negligible
Maximum elevation: 1380 m (4530 ft)
Maps: Gem Trek 1:35,000 Banff Up-Close and NTS 1:50,000 Banff 82-O/4
Trailhead: Midway along north side of Cave & Basin parking area, at intersection with footpath parallel to Cave Avenue 1.2 km from its start near the Bow River bridge at the south end of Banff Avenue.

0.0 — Trail intersection (elevation 1380 m). Descend slightly and head north along old levee.
0.4 — Sharp bend to the west to go along the south bank of the Bow River.
1.5 — *Sundance Canyon* trail (1380 m) at km 1.0.

The trail around the Cave & Basin Marsh is a relaxing saunter that provides an attractive choice if want to stretch the legs, for example after a visit to the National Historic Site. (The site has two adjacent short self-guiding boardwalk trails: one above, to the vent at the top of the Cave spring and to several small hotsprings; and one below to the marsh, where there is an observation blind. Another option is the 1.5 km long pedestrian trail along the north side of Cave Avenue between the site and the Bow River bridge.)

A muskrat might be glimpsed on this outing. This trail is one of the few in Banff National Park on which a wandering garter snake might be found—this completely harmless species is fully protected.

The birdlife at the marsh is similar to that at Vermilion Lakes, although usually not as abundant. A species commonly seen here is the ring-billed gull, with a black band around the bill near the tip. An interesting note is that although members of this subfamily are often referred to as seagulls, many spend much of their lives inland, nowhere near saltwater.

Wandering garter snake resting at Cave & Basin Marsh.

Sundance Canyon

Distance: 3.7 km (2.3 mi) — Cave & Basin to Sundance Canyon
Short hike: 45 minutes—1 hour one way
Elevation loss: 15 m (50 ft)
Elevation gain: 75 m (245 ft)
Maximum elevation: 1455 m (4770 ft)
Maps: Gem Trek 1:35,000 Banff Up-Close and NTS 1:50,000 Banff 82-O/4
Trailhead: West of the Cave & Basin National Historic Site, which is at the west end of Cave Avenue.

0.0 — Trail sign (elevation 1395 m). Head west on paved surface, descending gradually.
0.1 — Trailhead kiosk to right; keep straight.
0.6 — Keep straight (1385 m); *"Philosophers Knoll"* trail veers up to left.
1.0 — Keep straight (1380 m); *Cave & Basin Marsh* trail to right.
2.0 — Rest benches at Rainy Bay; view of Mt. Edith.
2.6 — Keep straight (1405 m); intersection with trail up west side of Sulphur Mountain to left and with trail to Healy Creek to right.
3.4 — Keep straight (1435 m); trail to Sundance Pass to left.
3.7 — End of paved trail at picnic area (1455 m).

Although this outing travels along a wide paved road and can be busy with other users (cyclists, rollerbladers, horseback riders, the occasional service vehicle), it is well worthwhile for the impressions it gives of a mountain valley—sensations that can be difficult to garner in Banff townsite.

A highlight is the section along the Bow River, reached after a gradual descent from the Cave & Basin. Here can be had an appreciation of how intimately linked the surrounding peaks are to the flowing water that helped create the valley and is still shaping it. It's also possible to imagine the long, deep tongues of slowly advancing ice that played a major role in sculpting the mountain landscape.

Two rest benches beside the backwater known as Rainy Bay are well situated for dramatic views of vertically-tilted Mt. Edith. If it's calm, the reflection adds to the sublimity of the scene. The area is noted for wildlife.

A four-way junction at km 2.6 presents three alternatives: to the left an old road leading up the west side of Sulphur Mountain in 5.4 km (3.3 mi), to the right a wide trail leading in 4.8 km (3.0 mi) to a bridge over Healy Creek near the Sunshine Road, and straight ahead the way to the picnic area.

Upon arrival at the tables and shelter, there is the option of taking a true foot-path to venture up a small canyon on Sundance Creek. After reaching the top of a series of waterfalls, the trail continues on a 2.1 km (1.3 mi) loop. It has some glimpses of the Sawback Range to the north from stands of lodgepole pine.

An 11.2 km (6.9 mi) extension, leaving the *Sundance Canyon* trail at km 3.4, allows a visit to Sundance Pass. The outing is rather uninspiring in terms of scenery, and the pass is difficult to distinguish because of its very gradual slope. The south end of this trail connects with the *Spray River* trail (possible seasonal closure) at km 6.0.

"Philosophers Knoll"

Distance: 2.1 km (1.3 mi) — Km 0.6 to km 2.6 of *Sundance Canyon* trail
Extension to short hike: 30—45 minutes one way
Elevation gain: 80 m (260 ft)
Elevation loss: 60 m (200 ft)
Maximum elevation: 1465 m (4805 ft)
Maps: Gem Trek 1:35,000 Banff Up-Close [side scramble unmarked] and NTS 1:50,000 Banff 82-O/4
Trailhead: Km 0.6 of *Sundance Canyon* trail (see p. 41).

0.0 — Sign at junction (elevation 1385 m). Head left up steep, wide dirt trail.
1.1 — Crest of trail (1465 m) just south of "Philosophers Knoll." (To ascend knoll, take faint path to north and scramble to summit.)
1.8 — Turn right and descend; left leads up Sulphur Mountain.
2.1 — Junction (1405 m) with km 2.6 of *Sundance Canyon* trail.

This knoll can be a quiet retreat from Banff townsite. As the unofficial name suggests, it is enough off the beaten track to often reward visitors with solitude, and the windy conditions often encountered are conducive to "clearing out the cobwebs."

The knoll provides a grand vista of the Bow Valley to the west. In addition to the often mesmerizing mountains, the river below sweeps by in a sinuous S-curve: a classic photographic composition.

Adventurous souls can take a steep rocky ridge down to the north to join the *Sundance Canyon* trail at approximately km 1.9. The standard continuation of this trail runs west from the crest to intersect an old track up the west side of Sulphur Mountain just 300 metres above the four-way junction at km 2.6 on the *Sundance Canyon* trail.

A firebreak and a prescribed burn at and above the crest at km 1.1 help reduce the risk of wildfire reaching Banff townsite. Other hazard-abatement measures have been performed or are planned for the Bow Valley area. Prescribed burns also help maintain ecological diversity. Vegetation regenerating after a prescribed burn can be seen on the *Muleshoe* trail (p. 154).

Bow River from "Philosophers Knoll."

Sulphur Mountain

Distance: 5.5 km (3.4 mi) — Upper Hot Springs to upper gondola terminal on Sulphur Mountain
Day hike: 2—2.5 hours one way
Elevation gain: 660 m (2165 ft)
Maximum elevation: 2260 m (7415 ft)
Maps: Gem Trek 1:35,000 Banff Up-Close and NTS 1:50,000 Banff 82-O/4
Trailhead: Steel gate across old road on final bend of the road leading to the Upper Hot Springs, just beyond junction for parking area at end of Mountain Avenue, 3.2 km (2.0 mi) from its beginning at junction with Spray Avenue 200 metres east of south end of Bow River bridge.

0.0 — Sign at gate at beginning of old access road (elevation 1600 m). Climb steadily on long zigzags, mostly below gondola line.
2.7 — Cement foundation of former resthouse.
5.5 — Upper gondola terminal (2260 m) on Sulphur Mountain.

The ridgecrest of Sulphur Mountain offers a widely recognized view of Banff townsite and its surroundings. A bonus of hiking up is a free gondola ride down (call (403) 762-2523 or 762-5438 {24-hour recorded message} for hours of operation).

Keep in mind that in spring there can still be lots of snow up high even if it's gone lower down.

The focal point of hikes up Sulphur Mountain is usually the restored weather observatory on nearby Sanson Peak. The name of that high point at the north end of long Sulphur Mountain honours Norman Sanson, curator of the Banff Park Museum from 1896 to 1931. Botanist John Macoun said that Sanson was "intelligent and well-educated [and] could talk natural history, geology, and anything else with the visitors."

Sanson climbed this trail up Sulphur Mountain regularly to take meteorological readings. On July 1, 1931, he was feted with a sunrise breakfast at the summit to mark one thousand ascents. Appropriately, given the great distances Sanson covered on foot, he was elected as the first president of the Skyline Trail Hikers in 1933.

An enjoyable ramble can be made south along the ridge from the upper gondola terminal. Here are found the subalpine larches growing closest to Banff townsite. The fairly well defined trail eventually fades just at a ledge whose traverse is not for anyone bothered by heights. The same applies to the granite-like boulders along the ridge, which can prove enjoyable for experienced scramblers.

The 5.4 km (3.3 mi) switchbacking trail on the west side of Sulphur Mountain links with the *Sundance Canyon* trail at km 2.6. This can serve as an alternate approach or allow a loop trip on this peak, which has many historical connotations. Besides the connections with Norman Sanson, Sulphur Mountain has cultural significance because of fissures in it that carry water heated at great depths up to a series of hotsprings...these thermal features led to the creation of what is now Banff National Park.

Bow Falls

Distance: 0.7 km (0.4 mi) — Glen Avenue east of the Bow River bridge to Bow
Falls
Walk: 15—20 minutes one way
Elevation gain: 10 m (33 ft)
Elevation loss: 20 m (65 ft)
Maximum elevation: 1390 m (4560 ft)
Maps: Gem Trek 1:35,000 Banff Up-Close and NTS 1:50,000 Banff 82-O/4
Trailhead: Glen Avenue, behind the YWCA, 100 metres east of south end of Bow
River bridge in Banff townsite. (A trail leads down to Glen Avenue from Spray
Avenue just east of the bridge; the west end of Glen Avenue goes through a tun-
nel under the south end of the bridge.)

0.0 — Keep straight on a wide old road (elevation 1380 m) where Glen Avenue
veers to the right; footpaths run parallel to this trail, closer to the south bank.
0.5 — Keep straight; old road turns right. Climb steps ahead to follow at edge of
cliff (1390 m) above Bow River.
0.7 — Descend to Bow Falls (1370 m).

This short, easy walk lies within the townsite but feels far removed from the
often frenetic pace of Banff Avenue. Start near the south end of the Bow River bridge,
with busts of a stylized Native chieftain on its cobblestone facade.

Follow east along the south bank of the Bow, whose seasonal character varies
from a surging, roiling, muddy brown torrent in spring flood to a tranquil, clear, turquoise river in late summer. These changes reflect the influence of warmer temperatures, first on the winter snowpack and later on the glaciers at the Bow's origin some
85 km to the northwest.

The finale to this outing is Bow Falls, where the river funnels through a rocky
gorge and dashes wildly over a total drop of some 10 metres. **Caution:** Don't go close
to the water or on adjacent cliffs.

**Swamp
currant
berries.**

Bow River

Distance: 1.3 km (0.8 mi) — East of Bow River bridge to canoe rental concession
Walk: 20—30 minutes one way
Elevation gain: Negligible
Maximum elevation: 1380 m (4530 ft)
Maps: Gem Trek 1:35,000 Banff Up-Close and NTS 1:50,000 Banff 82-O/4
Trailhead: In Banff townsite on south side of Buffalo Street (opposite south end of Beaver Street) 200 metres east of its intersection with Banff Avenue.

0.0 — Intersection (elevation 1380 m). Go south.

0.1 — Keep right; extension east, downstream along Bow River, reaches Tunnel Mountain Drive in 500 metres, along which it is possible to continue to a viewpoint for Bow Falls (where can connect with the trail below the south end of Tunnel Mountain to the *Bow River Hoodoos* trail; see p. 35).

0.3 — Pass under Bow River bridge; continue straight along river.

1.3 — Canoe rental concession on Bow Avenue near west end of Wolf Street (1380 m). It is possible to connect with the *Fenland* trail by continuing north and crossing the railway tracks, then turning left off the west side of Mount Norquay Road just 25 metres further north.

A trail follows along the Bow River from near the north end of the Banff Avenue bridge. This wide, paved, wheelchair accessible path can be joined at many points, including from Central Park (which has picnic tables and a gazebo). There are rest benches along the way, and interpretive signs.

Pileated woodpecker.

Lower Spray River

Distance: 11.1 km (6.9 mi) — Parking area near Banff Springs Hotel to Banff Springs Hotel golf course at first fairway
Day hike/backpack: 3—3.5 hours one way
Elevation gain: 50 m (165 ft)
Elevation loss: 75 m (250 ft)
Maximum elevation: 1450 m (4760 ft)
Maps: Gem Trek 1:35,000 Banff Up-Close and NTS 1:50,000 Banff 82-O/4
Trailhead: Gate at start of former fire road along west side of Spray River, reached by going straight under arch from end of Spray Avenue at Banff Springs Hotel.

0.0 — Trailhead kiosk (elevation 1400 m). Take wide gravel old road to south.

0.8 — Keep straight; path to left descends to footbridge over Spray River and up to km 9.9 of this trail.

2.0 — High point (1450 m).

5.5 — Turn left over footbridge (1430 m); *Spray River* trail to right.

6.3 — Backcountry campground.

7.5 — High point (1450 m).

9.9 — Keep straight; path to left leads to footbridge over Spray River and up to the junction at km 0.8.

10.4 — Keep straight (1415 m); *Mt. Rundle West Slope* trail to right. Descend gradually.

11.1 — Junction on south side of first fairway of Banff Springs Hotel golf course (1375 m). To link with the trailhead, take path north across golf course, turn west on road and cross bridge over Spray River, then take trail to left up past former clubhouse. An alternate, more direct link is via the path left at km 9.9.

Rosehip.

White-tailed deer.

The trails on both banks of the final stretch of the Spray River before its confluence with the Bow allow for a fairly long but mostly level circuit. There is the opportunity to stay overnight at a backcountry campground a mere 6 km from town. This loop is open to mountain biking.

The valley of the Spray is full of lodgepole pine, presently the most widespread conifer in the lower elevation forests of Banff National Park. Its success is due to an adaptation whereby its cones open in the heat of a fire to release their seeds. Many fires (most human caused) occurred in the area in the late 1800s; as a pioneer species that germinates readily after a burn, lodgepole pine now predominates. However, in the course of succession, shade tolerant trees such as spruce and Douglas-fir form the climax cover—though this is a slow process (taking a century or so) that can be altered if fire happens again. (And prescribed burns are now part of the picture.)

As its local common name implies, lodgepole pine has a straight growth form in the Rockies: a shape that made it useful for Native people in constructing shelters. However, there is a twist [pun warning] to the story, for this species was first described from specimens on the Pacific coast, where it is windswept and gnarled due to wind and salt spray. It is there commonly referred to as shore pine, and has the Latin name *Pinus contorta*, which doesn't jive with the Rockies subspecies.

The *Spray River* trail from the junction at km 5.5 continues to the Spray Lakes Reservoir (see p. 70).

The terrace at approximately km 10.1 gives a striking vantage upon the Banff Springs Hotel. If the trail between km 9.9 and km 0.8 is taken, rockclimbers might be seen in action on the practice cliffs of the old quarry near the footbridge.

Mt. Rundle West Slope

Distance: 5.5 km (3.4 mi) — *Lower Spray River* trail to end of established trail on Mt. Rundle
Day hike: 1.5—2 hours one way
Elevation gain: 585 m (1920 ft)
Maximum elevation: 2000 m (6560 ft)
Maps: Gem Trek 1:35,000 Banff Up-Close, and NTS 1:50,000 Banff 82-O/4 and Canmore 82-O/3
Trailhead: Km 10.4 of *Lower Spray River* trail (see p. 46). (This point is reached most directly from south side of first fairway of Banff Springs Hotel golf course in 700 metres.)

0.0 — Sign at junction (elevation 1415 m). Head east up steady switchbacks.
4.7 — Keep right; route to left climbs steeply toward subsidiary peak of Mt. Rundle.
5.5 — End of established trail (2000 m). Scrambling route toward northwest peak of Mt. Rundle crosses large gully and climbs very steeply.

Mt. Rundle, named after the Rev. Robert Rundle, an 1840s missionary in the area, is a landmark of Banff National Park whose image is widely associated with the Canadian Rockies. This trail on the west slopes of the mountain rises steadily through subalpine forest, switchbacking steeply in places and giving glimpses to the west and northwest before ending abruptly at a large gully.

If among the fair number of people keen on attempting the scramble to the northwest peak, be aware! Off-trail travel on Mt. Rundle is a serious undertaking, not to be taken lightly because of its ease of access. It requires confidence in moving over steep scree slopes, preparedness for changeable weather, and general alertness.

Least chipmunk.

Storm clouds clearing from Mt. Assiniboine and surrounding peaks, as seen from Mt. Rundle.

Parks Canada's Visitor Centre at 224 Banff Avenue has prepared a brochure that gives detailed background and a map of this scramble. To prevent an unnecessary tragedy, be informed and take this mountaineering endeavour seriously. Steer clear of this route if snow is going to be a problem. Taking out a voluntary safety registration might be a good idea, especially if solo (see p. 15).

To get on the route to the northwest peak—elevation 2949 m (9673 ft)—cross the gully. Don't go up the gully: it dead-ends at a headwall. Some hands-and-feet moves are called for to get up the far side of the gully into the forest, where there is a steep path up to the left. Eventually break out above the trees to a view of the summit. Realize, however, that it takes at least another hour to get to the top, and that en route there is a narrow rock rib with exposure to a fall.

A primitive rock wall at the summit gives some shelter. It's usually windy and cool up here: time to put on those extra layers. And take a drink. There's no water on the way, so bring lots of fluids and avoid dehydration.

All the precautions mentioned apply to the route up the subsidiary peak—elevation 2840 m (9315 ft)—that starts at the km 4.7 junction. If anything, this scramble is more technical, requiring a traverse below cliffbands before going up through a gap to the final steep incline. Be sure to go through this same notch on the way back.

These outings are not all rock and more rock. Least chipmunks, pikas, and Clark's nutcrackers occur above treeline. Roseroot, a rare high-elevation wildflower with succulent leaves, might capture attention. Even where the only plant life is a brilliant orange lichen (*Xanthoria* species), large black spiders can be found scuttling about.

Rundle Riverside

Distance: 8.0 km (5.0 mi) — Banff Springs Hotel golf course to Banff National Park boundary
Day hike: 2—2.5 hours one way
Elevation gain: 100 m (330 ft)
Elevation loss: 40 m (130 ft)
Maximum elevation: 1470 m (4820 ft)
Maps: Gem Trek 1:35,000 Banff Up-Close, and NTS 1:50,000 Banff 82-O/4 and Canmore 82-O/3
Trailhead: Trailhead kiosk at east end of Banff Springs Hotel golf course, reached by travelling east on road from bridge over Spray River near Bow Falls. [This road is closed in winter.]

0.0 — Trailhead kiosk (elevation 1370 m). Head east over undulating terrain.
4.9 — High point (1470 m).
8.0 — Banff National Park boundary (1430 m). Trail continues to Canmore Nordic Centre.

This rough trail runs from the Banff Springs Hotel golf course parallel to the Bow River, although it only passes beside the south bank for a short distance. It is mostly within forest but does cross a number of avalanche paths descending from the east face of Mt. Rundle. Mountain biking is permitted on this trail.

At the Banff National Park boundary, a surveyed line heads up toward cliffs—not feasible for hikers. The boundary runs toward the true summit of Mt. Rundle (not the northwest peak), then bends sharply to follow the ridge southeast.

American red squirrel.

Stoney Squaw

Distance: 2.3 km (1.4 mi) — Mt. Norquay Road to high point on Stoney Squaw
Day hike: 45 minutes—1 hour one way
Elevation gain: 185 m (610 ft)
Maximum elevation: 1880 m (6170 ft)
Maps: Gem Trek 1:35,000 Banff Up-Close and NTS 1:50,000 Banff 82-O/4
Trailhead: Immediately to right after turning off Mt. Norquay Road into large main parking area for downhill ski area, 6.0 km (3.7 mi) up the switchbacking road from the overpass above the Trans-Canada Highway.

0.0 — Sign (elevation 1695 m). Head into forest on steady climb.
2.3 — High point (1880 m) above east cliff of Stoney Squaw.

The name Stoney Squaw is in reference to the Stoney people who lived in the area before being 'relocated' to a reserve at Morley when Banff National Park was established. (This name may be changed in the future.) Mountain biking and horseback riding both take place on this trail.

The reward of views only comes near the end of this hike, but once at the bluff there is an expansive 180-degree panorama. The most eye-catching aspect of the scene is the south face of Cascade Mountain; in early summer, mountain goats may be seen on the rugged cliffs. It may come as a surprise that those sturdy alpine animals are found so close to Banff townsite; they are also at home on the east buttresses of Mt. Rundle.

Close examination of the rocks around trail's end on Stoney Squaw will reveal fossils, including of corals. (Don't disturb or remove any of these intriguing geological specimens.) Stoney Squaw is an example, like Tunnel Mountain, of a low peak that was entirely covered by ice during periods of glaciation.

An alternate route on the northern slopes of Stoney Squaw, most readily used on descent, passes through shady forest with a mossy floor before arriving at a ski run immediately east of and above the buildings of the Mt. Norquay ski area.

Fossil coral at end of Stoney Squaw trail.

Cascade Amphitheatre

Distance: 7.3 km (4.5 mi) — Mt. Norquay downhill ski area to Cascade
                                                                    Amphitheatre
Day hike: 2.5—3 hours one way
Elevation loss: 135 m (445 ft)
Elevation gain: 575 m (1890 ft)
Maximum elevation: 2135 m (7000 ft)
Maps: Gem Trek 1:35,000 Banff Up-Close and NTS 1:50,000 Banff 82-O/4
Trailhead: Northern end of main parking area of Mt. Norquay downhill ski area,
6.0 km (3.7 mi) up Mt. Norquay Road from the Norquay interchange on the Trans-
Canada Highway.

0.0 — Sign (elevation 1695 m). Head north, initially on asphalt surface between
ticket office and day lodge, then at base of ski runs.
0.6 — Keep straight; bridle path over footbridge to left.
0.7 — Keep straight (1680 m); *Forty Mile Creek* trail to left. Follow access road;
there is the option to pick up a less direct footpath behind the Spirit chair..
1.0 — Turn right just before base of Mystic chairlift (called Pathfinder Express in
2001) to pass behind {east of} it on boardwalk [may be damaged]. Come to a
Parks Canada sign in about 100 m [25 metres north of a small cinder block struc-
ture], where the trail leads into a narrow corridor through forest.
2.9 — Turn right; trail to left connects with *Forty Mile Creek* trail at km 3.3.
3.1 — Bridge over Forty Mile Creek (1560 m). Begin climbing.
4.3 — Turn right (1800 m); *Elk Pass* trail straight ahead. Ascend steeply.
7.3 — Cascade Amphitheatre (2135 m).

This energetic excursion is one that the author remembers well, having done
it in 1970 during his first summer of hiking in Banff National Park. He was a partici-
pant in the National Army Cadet Camp program, then based beneath Cascade Mountain. One reason the author recollects the outing vividly is that he was burdened with
additional weight in the form of bulky radio equipment.

Even if not carrying a heavy load, this is a demanding trip. One factor that
adds to the exertion is that the climb up to the amphitheatre begins by going down!
Yes: descend to Forty Mile Creek first. This goes so quickly when fresh that it might be
forgotten—until at day's end, when grinding back up the incline. In either direction,
wild onion with its nodding sprays of pinkish-lavender flowers can be seen along this
stretch in late July.

The real work begins at km 4.3, where this trail heads up a series of steep
switchbacks. The effort is rewarded with arrival at the amphitheatre, a glacially carved
cirque with typical high elevation wildlife such as pikas, marmots, and bighorn sheep.

White-tailed ptarmigan can also be met, feeding on the subalpine vegetation
in the meadows low in the bowl. Wildflowers bedeck the area through summer, the
species in bloom changing through the season.

If more ambitious, it's possible to try for the summit of Cascade Mountain,
whose elevation is 2998 m (9833 ft). As with Mt. Rundle, this is a demanding off-trail

Scramblers above Cascade Amphitheatre on the route toward the summit of Cascade Mountain.

scramble. Parks Canada's Visitor Centre at 224 Banff Avenue has prepared a brochure that gives detailed background and a map of this scramble.

The route goes via the west ridge: more or less the skyline as seen from Banff townsite. Veer back hard right from the amphitheatre (**don't** try to ascend the cirque walls) to pick up the route. There is a quasi-technical problem at a false summit, which must be turned on the right. Early in the season there will still be snow on the steep slope beneath the false summit: turn back if not comfortable with this kind of exposure. If do attempt to cross under these conditions, an ice axe is mandatory. In case of losing balance and beginning a slide, a self-arrest has to be executed (know how to do this beforehand!). Even later, when there is no snow, this traverse is airy.

If safely negotiate this obstacle, the final scree slope to the summit is easy. Don't become complacent, though, because there are still things to take into account. Like the big cornice to the right, which often hangs on [double meaning] through to autumn. Don't walk out on this—or on any other line of snow ending at sky—since it may break off and cause a fatal plunge.

The top of Cascade Mountain grants a superb view of Lake Minnewanka, and if into kite flying this is a great spot!

Elk Pass

Distance: 16.7 km (10.4 mi) — *Cascade Amphitheatre* trail to *Lower Cascade Valley* trail
Day hike/backpack: 2—2.5 hours to Elk Pass; 4.5—5 hours to Cascade Valley
Elevation gain: 260 m (850 ft)
Elevation loss: 420 m (1380 ft)
Maximum elevation: 2060 m (6760 ft)
Maps: Gem Trek 1:100,000 Banff & Mt. Assiniboine, and NTS 1:50,000 Banff 82-O/4 and Castle Mountain 82-O/5
Trailhead: Km 4.3 of *Cascade Amphitheatre* trail (see p. 52).

0.0 — Sign at junction (elevation 1800 m). Keep straight; *Cascade Amphitheatre* trail to right.

2.5 — Break out of forest into subalpine meadows.

7.2 — Keep right; trail straight ahead leads to Elk Lake in 2.2 km (1.4 mi). Back-country campground to left.

7.7 — Elk Pass (2060 m). Descend drainage to north.

13.7 — Footbridge across creek. Trail veers east in narrow gap between two high knolls of Cascade massif.

15.9 — Footbridge over Cascade River.

16.1 — Footbridge over Stony Creek. Trail leads northeast, parallel to Stony Creek (horse camp to southeast).

16.7 — *Lower Cascade Valley* trail (1640 m) at km 14.8.

The author at Elk Lake.

Rocky Mountain bighorn sheep lambs.

The meadows at Elk Pass make for an inviting destination, although reaching them entails a long approach through forest. En route from the Cascade Amphitheatre junction there are glimpses of the Brewster massif to the west. But it is the vista south from the meadows to Sulphur Mountain and beyond that makes the sweat and toil worthwhile.

Additional consolation if stay overnight at the backcountry campground could be sighting (as the author once did) several mule deer coming out of the forest in late evening to browse on the willows at the edge of the meadows.

The elk after which the features of this area are named may be in evidence; bighorn sheep [tan coats, light rump patches, brown horns] are almost guaranteed to be. Both these species are ungulates (cloven-hoofed), as are deer, moose, caribou, mountain goat, and bison.

An American kestrel, a small falcon with a distinctive whiskers-and-sideburns facial pattern, might also be sighted over the meadows. Formerly known as sparrow hawks, these birds often hover before dropping on small prey (mostly insects).

Having made the effort to reach Elk Pass, it's almost obligatory to visit Elk Lake. A 2.2 km (1.4 mi) trail that climbs 145 m (475 ft) leads to this colourful small tarn at the base of steep grey limestone walls.

The less-often used section of the *Elk Pass* trail (by those on foot, at least; horse traffic is quite heavy) drops north from the pass. It then bends east between two northern outliers of Cascade Mountain, crosses the Cascade River and Stony Creek on footbridges, and joins the *Lower Cascade Valley* trail.

A backpacking trip can be made on a 38.8 km (24.1 mi) loop using some or all of the Elk Pass, Stony Creek, and Cascade River backcountry campgrounds. This outing has a wilderness character despite its proximity to Banff townsite, as indicated by the presence of grizzly bears in the area.

Johnson Lake

Distance: 2.4 km (1.5 mi) — Circuit of Johnson Lake
Day hike: 30—45 minute loop
Elevation gain/loss: 10 m (33 ft)
Maximum elevation: 1420 m (4660 ft)
Maps: Gem Trek 1:35,000 Banff Up-Close and NTS 1:50,000 Canmore 82-O/3
Trailhead: Johnson Lake, reached by turning right at intersection 1.5 km (0.9 mi) north of Minnewanka interchange on Trans-Canada Highway, right again after a further 3.5 km (2.2 mi), and proceeding 2.0 km (1.2 mi) to parking area.

0.0 — Picnic area at northwest corner of Johnson Lake (elevation 1410 m). Follow the north shore, along paved trail at first, then make a sharp left turn after 100 metres to go around a cove on a dirt path that continues along open, south-facing slopes.

1.2 — Dam at east end of lake. Turn right at south end.

1.9 — High point (1420 m).

2.3 — Turn right to bridge over outlet at west end of lake.

2.4 — Return to picnic area (1410 m).

Prairie crocus.

This trail around Johnson Lake is now the only one open in the vicinity. A former network of other trails is no longer maintained by Parks Canada, in order to protect a secure area of montane habitat for wildlife. (The same applies to the former trail up Carrot Creek.)

The open south-facing slopes on the Johnson Lake circuit are especially good for wildflowers, including prairie crocus in early spring. A highlight of this area is the presence of numerous Douglas-fir trees, one of which—at about 700 years—is the oldest known example of the species in Alberta.

A picnic or even a swim can enhance this outing.

West end of Johnson Lake.

Bankhead

Distance: 1.1 km (0.7 mi) — Interpretive trail
Walk: 20—30 minute loop
Elevation loss/gain: 15 m (50 ft)
Maximum elevation: 1430 m (4690 ft)
Maps: Gem Trek 1:35,000 Banff Up-Close and NTS 1:50,000 Banff 82-O/4
Trailhead: Lower Bankhead parking area on east side of Lake Minnewanka Road, 3.2 km (2.0 mi) north of Minnewanka interchange on Trans-Canada Highway.

0.0 — Interpretive exhibit (elevation 1430 m). Descend stairs to large level area (1415 m) with remnants of coal mining buildings, and follow loop path.
1.1 — Climb stairs to return to parking area (1430 m).

This short interpretive trail gives an inkling of life in a coal mining community. Yes, there were mines within national parks, until a more ecologically oriented philosophy was enshrined in 1930 legislation. Until that time, park administrators actively supported this extractive industry because of the royalties it generated.

The Bankhead mine operated from 1903 to 1923, when the combination of increasingly difficult access to the seams deep inside Cascade Mountain, a sagging market, and a militant labour force led to its closure. The vibrant community that had grown up around the black fuel faded into dust, although many of the houses and public buildings were transported to Banff, Canmore, or Calgary. A lively and thorough account appears in the book *Bankhead—The Twenty Year Town* by Ben Gadd, published and distributed by the Friends of Banff National Park (see p. 19).

A 2.5 km (1.6 mi) trail follows the abandoned Bankhead railway line south to the Cascade Pond picnic area, which is reached by turning east off Lake Minnewanka Road 300 metres north of the Trans-Canada Highway.

Mule deer buck feeding on wild rose.

C-Level Cirque

Distance: 4.2 km (2.6 mi) — Upper Bankhead picnic area to C-Level Cirque
Day hike: 1.5—2 hours one way
Elevation gain: 450 m (1475 ft)
Maximum elevation: 1920 m (6300 ft)
Maps: Gem Trek 1:35,000 Banff Up-Close and NTS 1:50,000 Banff 82-O/4
Trailhead: Upper Bankhead picnic area, north off Lake Minnewanka Road
400 metres east of Lower Bankhead parking area.

0.0 — Sign (elevation 1470 m) at west end of parking area. Head straight into forest and begin steady climb.
1.1 — Cement shells of old mine buildings.
1.3 — Lake Minnewanka viewpoint at top of tailings pile just to the right off main trail.
1.9 — Abandoned mine ventilation shafts — fenced off for safety: no entrance.
4.2 — C-Level Cirque (1920 m).

Right from its start at the parking area where once stood the community of Upper Bankhead, this trail is intimately linked with the story of coal mining in Banff National Park. It passes by abandoned mine buildings and ventilation shafts (the latter fenced off for safety: stay away). The name of the trail comes from the level of a coal seam that was mined.

A huge tailings pile gives an expansive view east over Lake Minnewanka and to the Fairholme Range, and south to Mt. Rundle. Incongruously, calypso orchids now blossom on this black heap, showing that natural regeneration can be surprising.

A faint trail continues up north from the small pool at the lip of the cirque, gaining a small, larch-crowned knoll.

Snow often persists on the shady lower parts of this trail until well into summer. Avalanches occur in the cirque during hiking season.

This hike is best done in the morning before the sun disappears behind the cliffs of Cascade Mountain, particularly if want to take photographs.

Lower Cascade Valley

Distance: 15.2 km (9.4 mi) — Upper Bankhead picnic area to junction with
Dormer Pass and River trail
Day hike/backpack: 4—5 hours one way
Elevation gain: 240 m (785 ft)
Elevation loss: 70 m (230 ft)
Maximum elevation: 1670 m (5480 ft)
Maps: Gem Trek 1:100,000 Banff & Mt. Assiniboine, and NTS 1:50,000 Banff 82-O/4
and Castle Mountain 82-O/5
Trailhead: As for *C-Level Cirque* trail (see p. 59).

0.0 — Trailhead kiosk (elevation 1470 m) at east end of parking area. Take trail starting through meadow.
1.2 — Turn left up former Cascade fire road; old access road to right.
5.1 — Crest (1585 m) before descent to Cascade River.
6.4 — Keep right; straight ahead is ford used by horse parties.
6.5 — Footbridge over Cascade River (1545 m). Backcountry campground to west on north side of bridge. Continue north on former fire road: level at first, then over undulating terrain.
12.0 — High point (1670 m).
13.2 — Keep straight; trail to left leads to warden cabins.
14.2 — Keep straight over level section; trail back hard left leads to warden cabins, trail to left leads to horse camp.
14.8 — Keep straight; *Elk Pass* trail to left.
15.0 — Footbridge over Stony Creek (1640 m).
15.2 — Sign (1640 m). Backcountry campground and *Dormer Pass and River* trail to east; *Upper Cascade Valley* trail to north.

This trail along a former fire road is rather mundane, but it is quick and does give views of the peaks on either side of the valley. On the east is the Palliser Range, while to the west runs the long spine of Cascade Mountain. (This trail up to km 15.0 is open to mountain bikes.)

The Cascade River is not reached until km 6.5, where a high bridge crosses the wide channel. Continuing north, the trail stays level and close to the river for a couple of kilometres. Then it rolls up and down small hills before dropping to the flats 800 metres before the Stony Creek bridge.

This area is good elk habitat and so attracts grizzly bears. The author had a close call with one about 500 metres east of the Stony Creek backcountry campground in late June, 1989. He climbed a tree, and so did the bear—putting to rest the notion that no grizzly can do so. This was a subadult, but nevertheless big enough to cause some anxious moments when it clambered up to within a metre. Luckily the tree was tall enough that the author was able to get 11 m off the ground, which is the minimum distance recommended by Herrero (see p. 20). So the incident ended without any harm done. {Keep in mind that even though an adult grizzly cannot climb very well because of its weight, it can easily reach up to 3 m high.}

Coyote.

This is a reminder to take all precautions, here and everywhere in the Rockies. Certainly heed any bear warnings or area closures.

A non-threatening yet no less fascinating species that may also be sighted on this trail is the coyote. This resourceful and adaptable creature is important in the mythology of Native people, who know it as *meschachakan* ("the versatile").

Near the end of this trail are three possible continuations. To the west is the *Elk Pass* trail, to the east the *Dormer Pass and River* trail, while to the north the *Upper Cascade Valley* trail continues into the remote northeastern sector of Banff National Park.

Lake Minnewanka

Distance: 29.5 km (18.3 mi) — Lake Minnewanka parking area to Devils Gap
Walk/day hike/backpack: 30 minutes one way to Stewart Canyon,
                       9—10 hours one way to Devils Gap
Elevation gain: 85 m (280 ft)
Elevation loss: 45 m (150 ft)
Maximum elevation: 1525 m (5000 ft)
Maps: Gem Trek 1:100,000 Banff & Mt. Assiniboine, and NTS 1:50,000 Lake Minnewanka 82-O/6 and Canmore 82-O/3
Trailhead: Lake Minnewanka parking area off Lake Minnewanka Road 5.5 km (3.4 mi) from the Trans-Canada Highway interchange, north of the dam at the east end of the lake.

0.0 — Gate on service road at concession (elevation 1480 m). Take paved road through picnic area.
0.6 — Pavement ends at turning loop. Hiking path begins between trailhead kiosk and trail sign.
1.5 — Bridge over Cascade River at Stewart Canyon (marked incorrectly on the Castle Mountain 1:50,000 NTS map, sheet 82-O/5). Main trail veers up left after crossing bridge, then turns right to go over a ridge and drop to the lake.
7.8 — Keep straight (1480 m); *Aylmer Pass* trail to left and backcountry campground to right.
9.3 — Backcountry campground.
11.1 — Backcountry campground.
18.8 — Backcountry campground.
20.1 — Backcountry campground.
20.4 — Trail cuts northeast away from lakeshore.
22.8 — East end of Lake Minnewanka.
23.8 — First Ghost Lake.
25.6 — Keep east after ford (1495 m) between First and Second Ghost lakes; rough trail to west runs about 9 km (5.5 mi) along south shore to a dead end. This trail may be delisted by the park in the future, and the backcountry campground 3.0 km along it may be removed. (The former trail to Carrot Creek is no longer maintained, in order to protect a secure area of montane habitat for wildlife).
27.6 — Third Ghost Lake.
29.5 — Park boundary in Devils Gap (1520 m). Trail continues east on provincial land.

     The short walk to the bridge above the Cascade River at Stewart Canyon—named after Banff National Park's first superintendent—is a pleasant saunter, along which it is virtually guaranteed to see bighorn sheep. (Leave them wild; don't treat them like pets or zoo specimens by feeding or enticing.)
     The trail along the north shore of Lake Minnewanka follows in reverse the route taken by Sir George Simpson, Governor of the Hudson's Bay Company, on a round-the-world journey in 1841. (He didn't have mountain bikes, which are an

Lake Minnewanka and reflections, including of Cascade Mountain on the right.

option now. Neither did he have motorboats, which are allowed on the lake.)

There are five backcountry campgrounds along the north shore. The trail passes through areas regenerating after a prescribed burn in 1988. Hiking this trail gives a firsthand impression of the curving shape of the lake, and affords continually new views as progressing eastward. Particularly striking are the summits of the Fairholme Range to the south: Inglismaldie, Girouard, and Peechee—this last named in honour of Simpson's Native guide.

The Stoney people knew this lake as *Minnewanka*, which has been translated as "Water of the Spirits." This illustrates the profound significance they attached to it. Aboriginal artifacts from the area indicate occupation as far back as 11,000 years ago.

A school of fingerlings might be seen swimming in the shallows, one of which might grow into a huge lake trout. The odds, though, are that most will end up in the stomach of a predator such as a loon or a merganser. The maximum recorded depth of Lake Minnewanka is almost 100 metres (330 feet).

The trail skirts the south sides of the two lower, intermittent Ghost Lakes to arrive at the park boundary in Devils Gap, below the brooding cliffs of Phantom Crag. This area features active dunes of material blown from the often dry lake beds by the prevailing westerlies. These aeolian (from Aeolus, Greek god of the winds) deposits have reached to 1.5 metres up the trunks of living trees.

Aylmer Pass

Distance: 5.7 km (3.5 mi) — *Lake Minnewanka* trail to Aylmer Pass
Day hike/backpack: 2—2.5 hours one way
Elevation gain: 800 m (2620 ft)
Maximum elevation: 2280 m (7480 ft)
Maps: Gem Trek 1:100,000 Banff & Mt. Assiniboine and NTS 1:50,000 Lake Minnewanka 82-O/6
Trailhead: Km 7.8 of *Lake Minnewanka* trail (see p. 62).

0.0 — Sign at junction (elevation 1480 m). Head north up steep trail.
2.3 — Keep straight; trail to right leads to site of former Aylmer fire lookout tower [elevation 2050 m (6725 ft)] in 1.7 km (1.1 mi).
5.7 — Open alpine terrain of Aylmer Pass (2280 m).

The ascent to Aylmer Pass from Lake Minnewanka is a demanding outing involving an average 14 percent grade. So sighting bighorn sheep, which is quite likely, can be good reason to take a breather. Patience might be rewarded with observation of rams clashing. **Note:** Cougar frequent the area.

The pass features alpine meadows and views north into the provincially administered Ghost River Wilderness Area (backpacking destination). A popular trip, either in conjunction with a visit to Aylmer Pass or by itself, is the jaunt to the site of a former fire lookout tower on the ridge to the east. The well-designed, more gradual spur trail leads to an inspiring view of Lake Minnewanka far below.

The truly energetic can pursue the ascent of Mt. Aylmer, either along the sharp ridge north of the lookout site (one detour to the east to avoid gable ends) or via a steep scramble up from the pass. Once the final scree slopes are surmounted, Lake Minnewanka lies spread out below as if in a photograph taken with a fisheye lens (see p. 18). The summit, whose elevation is 3163 m (10,375 ft), stands out from the surrounding peaks and grants an excellent panorama.

Mt. Aylmer was named by J.J. McArthur, who made the first ascent, after his hometown in the province of Quebec. It stands as the highest point within a 30 km radius of Banff townsite.

Rocky Mountain bighorn rams clashing (photographed on *Aylmer Pass* trail).

Edith Pass

Distance: 6.9 km (4.3 mi) — Fireside picnic area to *Forty Mile Creek* trail
Day hike: 2—2.5 hours one way
Elevation gain: 510 m (1675 ft)
Elevation loss: 270 m (890 ft)
Maximum elevation: 1945 m (6380 ft)
Maps: Gem Trek 1:35,000 Banff Up-Close and NTS 1:50,000 Banff 82-O/4
Trailhead: Fireside picnic area, reached by taking turnoff onto the Bow Valley
Parkway (Highway 1A) 5.5 km (3.4 mi) west of Mt. Norquay interchange on the
Trans-Canada Highway, then turning right after 0.5 km (0.3 mi) and going 1.0 km
(0.6 mi) to parking area at end of narrow road.

0.0 — Trailhead kiosk (elevation 1435 m). Cross footbridge to large fireplace and
take old roadway east.
0.2 — Veer left onto narrow footpath and contour through montane (low elevation) forest of conifers and trembling aspen.
1.1 — Keep straight (1470 m); *Cory Pass* trail to left.
1.3 — Turn left; old trail to right leads to fence above highway. Climb steadily.
4.0 — Keep straight (1860 m); *Cory Pass* trail to left.
4.6 — Edith Pass (1945 m). Descend steadily.
6.8 — Footbridge over Forty Mile Creek.
6.9 — Intersection (1675 m) with *Forty Mile Creek* trail at km 5.3.

This trail connects the Bow Valley and that of Forty Mile Creek, but it is
most often used in part on a loop with the *Cory Pass* trail. The most appealing part of
the trail is the early stage through a stand of trembling aspens.

The first spring foliage of these deciduous trees is refreshingly green after a
season of white, their full summer raiment can provide welcome shade, while the fall
colours of yellow and some red are dazzlingly beautiful.

The remainder of the trail is within enclosed coniferous forest that doesn't
provide much in the way of views, though it can have its own rewards.

Edith Pass and Mt.
Edith (left) and Mt.
Brewster from *Cory
Pass* trail.

Cory Pass

Distance: 7.9 km (4.9 mi) — Km 1.1 to km 4.0 of *Edith Pass* trail
Day hike: 3.5—4 hours one way
Elevation gain: 890 m (2920 ft)
Elevation loss: 500 m (1640 ft)
Maximum elevation: 2360 m (7740 ft)
Maps: Gem Trek 1:35,000 Banff Up-Close and NTS 1:50,000 Banff 82-O/4
Trailhead: Km 1.1 of *Edith Pass* trail (see p. 65).

0.0 — Junction (elevation 1470 m). Head north up very steep trail.

1.3 — Gain crest of south ridge of Mt. Edith. Climb more gradually, with a short descent at notch before beginning traverse across open slopes toward pass.

4.7 — Cory Pass (2360 m). To continue, descend steeply into Gargoyle Valley and keep close to north cliffs of Mt. Edith. There is one section of climbing before descent on switchbacks.

7.9 — Intersection (1860 m) with *Edith Pass* trail at km 4.0.

This strenuous hike goes high and gives a feeling of escape from the daily grind. The way indicated above is the most direct approach to Cory Pass. Head steeply up a grassy slope interspersed with aspens, then plunge into forest before gaining the south ridge of Mt. Edith.

Just before reaching the rocky southwest slopes of the mountain, descend a short rock step, then traverse toward Cory Pass. (Don't drop east toward Edith Pass from the rock step; if doing this loop in the opposite direction to this description, be aware that have to climb up this short bit to continue the descent.)

Purple saxifrage.

Silhouettes at Cory Pass.

The final stretch toward the pass weaves in and out of a series of gullies, A highlight of this section in early summer is the purple saxifrage that will be found in bloom.

To make a circuit, descend north from Cory Pass, staying high and close to the sheer base of Mt. Edith. (Don't follow the drainage down toward Forty Mile Creek, as the author did his first time on this trail, when snow obscured the route.) Be alert for a short spate of climbing up an avalanche chute, and look for flagging tape on trees at its east edge to pick up the trail that switchbacks down to the *Edith Pass* trail.

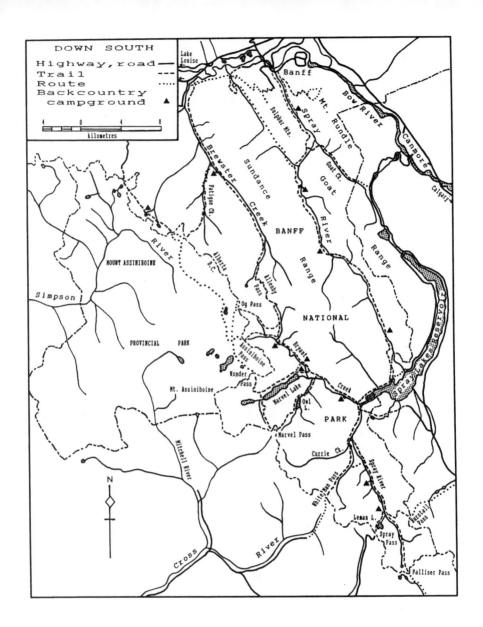

Down South

Spray River, with Sulphur Mountain (left) and Mt. Rundle, from the backcountry campground at km 10.9 of the *Spray River* trail.

Spray River

Distance: 39.1 km (24.2 mi) — *Lower Spray River* trail to *Bryant Creek* trail
Backpack: 2—2.5 days one way
Elevation gain: 340 m (1115 ft)
Elevation loss: 50 m (165 ft)
Maximum elevation: 1770 m (5800 ft)
Maps: Gem Trek 1:100,000 Banff & Mt. Assiniboine, and NTS 1:50,000 Banff 82-O/4, Canmore 82-O/3, and Spray Lakes Reservoir 82 J/14
Trailhead: Km 5.5 of *Lower Spray River* trail (see p. 46).

0.0 — Sign (elevation 1430 m). Head south, up Spray Valley.

2.4 — Keep straight; old logging road (dead end) to left.

4.1 — Keep straight (1520 m); *Goat Creek* trail to left.

4.5 — Keep straight; site of former warden cabin down to left. Pass between Sulphur Mountain and Goat Range.

6.0 — Keep straight; trail to Sundance Pass to right.

10.9 — Backcountry campground.

17.2 — Backcountry campground and warden cabin.

17.6 — Footbridge over Spray River.

24.0 — High point (1770 m).

29.3 — Backcountry campground.

29.5 — Footbridge over Spray River.

30.3 — Keep left; warden cabin to right [no longer used and may be removed].

31.7 — Gate; cross out of Banff National Park.

33.2 — Keep right; Canyon Dam 1.8 km to left. Follow along north shore of Spray Lakes Reservoir.

38.0 — Re-enter Banff National Park at access gate.

38.9 — Keep straight; footbridge over Bryant Creek to left.

39.1 — Junction (1720 m) with *Bryant Creek* trail at km 6.4.

This trail passes through prime wildlife territory. Grizzly bears and wolves use this area, as do their prey species such as elk, bighorn sheep, and mountain goat (especially the meadows on the Goat Range to the east.) There may be a seasonal closure.

Mt. Turbulent is passed en route to the backcountry campground at km 29.3, which is named after the more auspiciously christened Mt. Fortune. A gravel flat shortly beyond marks the gorge leading to Canyon Dam. The trail makes an S-turn and bypasses a small, old warden cabin [may be removed] before reaching a gate at the national park boundary.

The last section of this old fire road hugs the shore of the artificially created Spray Lakes Reservoir before arriving at what Parks Canada calls Trail Centre. This important junction offers several choices: the *Bryant Creek* trail toward Mt. Assiniboine or out to the Mt. Shark trailhead, or the *Palliser Pass* trail south.

Goat Creek

Distance: 8.4 km (5.2 mi) — *Spray River* trail to Banff National Park boundary
Day hike: 2—2.5 hours one way
Elevation loss: 10 m (33 ft)
Elevation gain: 145 m (475 ft)
Maximum elevation: 1655 m (5430 ft)
Maps: Gem Trek 1:100,000 Banff & Mt. Assiniboine, and NTS 1:50,000 Banff 82-O/4 and Canmore 82-O/3
Trailhead: Km 4.1 of *Spray River* trail.

0.0 — Sign (elevation 1520 m). Descend to east.
0.3 — Cross footbridge (1510 m) over Spray River.
2.2 — Cross footbridge over Goat Creek.
8.4 — Banff National Park boundary (1655 m). Trail continues to Smith-Dorrien/Spray Trail (road) in 1.5 km.

This spur off the *Spray River* trail is a straightforward ascent (open to mountain bikes) to the Banff National Park boundary between the southeast end of Mt. Rundle and the Goat Range. There is an unusual view of Mt. Rundle from the bridge at km 2.2; below is a small waterfall cascading over sedimentary rock layers.

An interesting loop of over 40 km (25 mi) can be made by using this trail, the Spray River routes, the *Rundle Riverside* trail, and sections of trail and road outside the national park. This completes a circumnavigation of the long chain of peaks that constitutes Mt. Rundle.

Small waterfall over ledge below footbridge at km 2.2 of *Goat Creek* trail.

Brewster Creek

Distance: 27.6 km (17.1 mi) — Sunshine Road to Allenby Pass
Backpack: 1.5—2 days one way
Elevation gain: 1015 m (3330 ft)
Maximum elevation: 2435 m (7985 ft)
Maps: Gem Trek 1:100,000 Banff & Mt. Assiniboine, and NTS 1:50,000 Banff 82-O/4 and Mount Assiniboine 82 J/13
Trailhead: Parking area on east side of Sunshine Road, 0.8 km (0.5 mi) off the Sunshine interchange on the Trans-Canada Highway, which is 9.0 km (5.6 mi) west of the Mt. Norquay Road overpass.

0.0 — Trailhead kiosk (elevation 1420 m) at east end of parking area. Head east across footbridge over Healy Creek and along old roadway.

0.9 — Turn right up steep narrow path. This shortcut saves 1.9 km of travel; to keep to the more gradual road, continue straight to a junction 1.2 km farther east and turn right. (This junction is 2.9 km from the four-way intersection at km 2.6 of the *Sundance Canyon* trail.)

1.3 — Rejoin wide roadway.

9.2 — Outfitter's lodge. Keep straight; trail narrows.

10.8 — Keep straight (1615 m); *Fatigue Creek* trail to right.

13.2 — Cross Brewster Creek.

23.5 — Outfitter's lodge; cross footbridge south of lodge.

24.3 — Begin steep switchbacking ascent.

27.6 — Allenby Pass (2435 m).

This trail (though not the shortcut described above) is more often used by horse parties or mountain bikers than by hikers or backpackers. The ascent of Brewster Creek is of historical interest in that it was long the route between Banff and the Mt. Assiniboine area, used for example in walking tours operated by A.O. Wheeler in the 1920s.

Especially from the open area near the headwaters of the creek, there are good views of the serrated peaks of the Sundance Range and of the isolated Brewster Glacier. The trail does not go toward the ice, however, rather taking the tributary valley southwest before commencing the very steep ascent to Allenby Pass.

Call (403) 762-4551 for information on the two lodges on this route, or write Sundance Lodge, P.O. Box 2280, Banff, Alberta, Canada T0L 0C0.

Brewster Glacier from *Brewster Creek* trail.

Fatigue Creek

Distance: 11.3 km (7.0 mi) — *Brewster Creek* trail to Fatigue Pass
Backpack: 6—7 hours one way
Elevation gain: 825 m (2710 ft)
Maximum elevation: 2440 m (8000 ft)
Maps: Gem Trek 1:100,000 Banff & Mt. Assiniboine and NTS 1:50,000 Banff 82-O/4
Trailhead: Km 10.8 of *Brewster Creek* trail.

0.0 — Sign at junction (elevation 1615 m). Head right (south).
0.2 — Ford Brewster Creek to west bank.
1.1 — First of six fords of Fatigue Creek in next 4 km. Steady ascent up valley.
11.3 — Fatigue Pass (2440 m) and Banff National Park boundary. The south end of the *Citadel Pass* trail is 2.5 km to northwest (see p. 92)

This seldom-used trail lives up to its name, for it involves numerous fords. Its redeeming feature is the high pass at its head (although this is much more readily visited via the *Citadel Pass* trail).

Despite the unappealing name, it is possible to climb Fatigue Mountain—elevation 2959 m (9707 ft)—just expect a tiresome toil up scree slopes.

Fatigue Mountain from Fatigue Pass.

Bryant Creek

Distance: 22.7 km (14.1 mi) — Mt. Shark trailhead in Kananaskis Country to Assiniboine Pass
Backpack: 1.5—2 days one way
Elevation gain: 520 m (1705 ft)
Elevation loss: 105 m (345 ft)
Maximum elevation: 2180 m (7150 ft)
Maps: Gem Trek 1:100,000 Banff & Mt. Assiniboine, and NTS 1:50,000 Spray Lakes Reservoir 82 J/14 and Mount Assiniboine 82 J/13
Trailhead: Mt. Shark parking area at end of 4.6 km (2.9 mi) spur road west off Smith-Dorrien/Spray Trail (road) at junction 37 km (23 mi) south of the bridge over the Bow River in Canmore (the road is gravel from 1 km (0.6 mi) beyond the Nordic Centre, and narrow and winding in places).

0.0 — Trailhead kiosk (elevation 1765 m). Take short path leading to gated road; travel through logged area.

3.6 — Keep straight (1800 m); Watridge Lake to left. Descend, gradually at first, then more steeply.

5.8 — Cross footbridge over Spray River (1705 m) and turn right; *Palliser Pass* trail to left.

6.1 — High point (1720 m).

6.3 — Cross footbridge (1710 m) over Bryant Creek and turn left; trail to right leads to *Spray River* trail in 200 metres.

6.4 — Turn left (1720 m); *Spray River* trail to right.

6.7 — Keep straight; warden cabin to left.

9.3 — Backcountry campground; cross tributary stream on footbridge.

11.7 — Keep straight (1770 m); *Owl Lake* trail to left.

12.7 — Keep straight (1795 m); backcountry campground (600 metres) and *Marvel Lake* and *Wonder Pass* trails to left.

13.3 — Keep straight; Bryant Creek trail shelter 200 metres to left.

14.0 — Keep straight. Backcountry campground and warden cabin to right; connector (1.1 km long) to *Marvel Lake* and *Wonder Pass* trails to left.

16.9 — Backcountry campground.

17.2 — Keep right; horse trail ford straight ahead.

17.4 — Cross Allenby Creek on footbridge.

17.7 — Keep left (1900 m); *Allenby Pass* trail to right. Begin traverse above north side of Bryant Creek.

22.1 — Keep right; horse trail comes in from left. Ascend steep switchbacks.

22.7 — Assiniboine Pass (2180 m) and Alberta/British Columbia boundary. Trail continues west into B.C.'s Mount Assiniboine Provincial Park.

This trail up the valley of Bryant Creek in Banff National Park is one of the premier backpacking routes in the Canadian Rockies. After passing between the precipitous portals of Mt. Turner and Cone Mountain, there is a backcountry campground at km 9.3. The junction with the *Owl Lake* trail is 2.4 km farther on.

Scene on upper stretch of *Bryant Creek* trail.

A gradual ascent sees arrival in the vicinity of three possible overnight camping spots: two backcountry campgrounds and the park-operated Bryant Creek trail shelter. Trails to Marvel Lake turn off here, connecting with the *Wonder Pass* trail into Mount Assiniboine Provincial Park. The approach via Assiniboine Pass is easier, but a recommended loop returns to Marvel Lake via Wonder Pass (if it's not closed due to bear activity).

Farther up Bryant Creek is a level marshy area (trail sometimes wet) where moose might be sighted. After another backcountry campground, arrive at a junction. A swift ford here is used by horse parties, who take a route to the pass that is more direct but which requires several more stream crossings.

The hiker trail leads away from Bryant Creek, then in just 200 metres crosses Allenby Creek. Keep left at the junction with the *Allenby Pass* trail and climb steadily on an arc that connects with the horse trail. Clamber up through rockbands to Assiniboine Pass, the threshold for Mount Assiniboine Provincial Park.

Palliser Pass

Distance: 20.7 km (12.8 mi) — *Bryant Creek* trail to Palliser Pass
Backpack: 1—1.5 day(s) one way
Elevation gain: 395 m (1295 ft)
Maximum elevation: 2100 m (6890 ft)
Maps: Gem Trek 1:100,000 Banff & Mt. Assiniboine and NTS 1:50,000 Spray Lakes Reservoir 82 J/14 and Kananaskis Lakes 82 J/11
Trailhead: Km 5.8 of *Bryant Creek* trail (see p. 74).

0.0 — Sign (elevation 1705 m) west of Spray River footbridge. Turn south; north leads up Bryant Creek.

2.5 — Keep right; ford straight ahead.

3.2 — Turn left and cross footbridge over Currie Creek (1750 m); to right is *White Man Pass* trail.

3.6 — Cross footbridge over Spray River and turn right. Steady climb.

6.8 — Keep straight; cut-off (2.0 km) to *White Man Pass* trail to right [tricky ford].

9.3 — Backcountry campground.

9.5 — Enter meadows; warden cabin off to left.

9.8 — Cross Birdwood Creek on footbridge.

13.3 — Keep east on bench trail to avoid wet sections.

14.0 — Keep straight (1875 m); *Spray Pass* trail and backcountry campground (100 metres) to right.

15.0 — Keep straight (1900 m); *Burstall Pass* trail to left.

18.6 — Steep ascent for 1 km.

19.9 — East shore of Belgium Lake.

20.7 — Palliser Pass (2100 m) and Alberta/B.C. boundary. Trail/route continues south down Palliser Valley in Height of the Rockies Provincial Park.

The uppermost part of the long valley of the Spray River (part of which was inundated by the Spray Lakes Reservoir) remains an unspoiled wilderness area thanks to its inclusion in Banff National Park, although there are several encroachments from the west.

Boreal owl photographed along *Palliser Pass* trail.

Peaks in vicinity of Spray Pass reflected in pool on Spray River.

Head up the west side of the Spray River from the trailhead, reaching open meadows in a little over two kilometres. The first junction with the *White Man Pass* trail is another kilometre or so farther. Taking two footbridges that obviate the need for a ford, cross to the east side of the Spray and gain some 60 metres of elevation over the next 2 km.

It was along this stretch on a 1988 visit that the author had the privilege of seeing a boreal owl, a species that—like the spotted owl—requires old-growth forest. The bird stayed on its perch, and allowed a quiet approach to take photographs.

Farther upvalley are vast flat meadows before the junctions with the *Spray Pass* and *Burstall Pass* trails. Onward are more of the attractive, level meadows that fill the valley bottom, the river winding through on a meandering course.

The final section to Palliser Pass climbs 150 metres up a wooded slope to emerge in subalpine surroundings. Travel along the east shore of small Belgium Lake to reach the pass, indicated by an old survey marker. This is the southernmost point in Banff National Park.

From the pass a rough trail with difficult fords continues south on the west side of the Palliser River. After approximately 5 km a side trail climbs steeply to North Kananaskis Pass and so to Upper Kananaskis Lake.

White Man Pass

Distance: 7.7 km (4.8 mi) — *Palliser Pass* trail to White Man Pass
Day hike/backpack: 2.5—3.5 hours one way
Elevation gain: 400 m (1310 ft)
Maximum elevation: 2150 m (7050 ft)
Maps: Gem Trek 1:100,000 Banff & Mt. Assiniboine and NTS 1:50,000 Spray Lakes Reservoir 82 J/14
Trailhead: Km 3.2 of *Palliser Pass* trail (see p. 76).

0.0 — Sign (elevation 1750 m). Head southwest up valley of Currie Creek.
1.3 — Ford Currie Creek.
1.6 — Ford White Man Creek.
3.9 — Keep straight; to left is 2.0 km shortcut joining *Palliser Pass* trail at km 6.8. [The ford of the Spray River on this shortcut can be deep and swift.]
5.6 — Cross small stream beyond end of meadow; begin steep climb. There are two unmarked junctions on the way up: go right at the first and left at the second.
7.2 — Small unnamed lake in zone of subalpine larch.
7.7 — White Man Pass (2150 m) and Alberta/British Columbia boundary. Trail continues west to join a logging road on the Cross River in approximately 6 km.

White Man Pass is little visited nowadays, yet it was one of the earlier places in Banff National Park to be reached by non-Natives. A party of westbound emigrants led by James Sinclair was guided over the pass in 1841 by Maskepetoon, a Cree chief. The hardy pioneers even took cattle with them on their gruelling journey.

The Jesuit missionary Father Pierre Jean de Smet crossed the continental divide via White Man Pass in 1845, and wrote of the area that "all was wild sublimity." A wooden cross erected at the time gave rise to the name of the Cross River, which flows west from the pass. It is thought that the original Native name of the pass refers to de Smet's visit.

Bunchberry.

Looking east from outlet of lake below White Man Pass toward meadows on White Man Creek and peaks beyond—Mt. Nestor (left) and Mt. Shark (right).

Other salient figures in the chronicles of Rockies exploration passed through this saddle, including British military officers Henry James Warre and Mervin Vavasour (who were guided by fur trader Peter Skene Ogden on their secret reconnaissance mission), geologist George M. Dawson in his determined efforts to thoroughly map the region, and the indomitable Major A.B. Rogers during his search for a railroad route to the West Coast.

Tracing the footsteps of these predecessors gives admiration for their pluck and perseverance, especially since the country can be experienced much as they did.

In this wilderness area, there is the chance of witnessing a magnificent golden eagle soaring along the cliffs of Mt. Currie, and of seeing sunlight sparkling on multi-hued wildflowers speckled with morning dew.

Spray Pass

Distance: 2.2 km (1.4 mi) — *Palliser Pass* trail to Spray Pass
Day hike: 30—45 minutes one way
Elevation loss: 30 m (100 ft)
Elevation gain: 90 m (295 ft)
Maximum elevation: 1960 m (6430 ft)
Maps: Gem Trek 1:100,000 Banff & Mt. Assiniboine, and NTS 1:50,000 Spray Lakes Reservoir 82 J/14 and Kananaskis Lakes 82 J/11
Trailhead: Km 14.0 of *Palliser Pass* trail (see p. 76).

0.0 — Sign (elevation 1875 m). Descend to southwest.
0.1 — Cross Spray River (1870 m). Backcountry campground; climb steadily to southwest.
1.1 — North end of Leman Lake. Continue along west shore.
1.6 — High point (1960 m).
2.2 — Spray Pass (1935 m) and Alberta/British Columbia boundary. Logging road reaches almost to pass from west.

This short spur off the *Palliser Pass* trail gives access to low, forested Spray Pass on the continental divide. (A logging road reaches almost to the pass.)

The trail to the pass runs along the north shore of Leman Lake, a brilliant gem in an impressive setting complemented by surrounding peaks including Mt. Leman, Mt. Leval, and Mt. Sir Douglas.

Leman Lake can easily be circumnavigated via its south shore in a variation involving a bit of scrambling.

South over Leman Lake toward Mt. Sir Douglas from *Spray Pass* trail.

Burstall Pass

Distance: 3.5 km (2.2 mi) — *Palliser Pass* trail to Burstall Pass
Day hike/backpack: 1.5—2 hours one way
Elevation gain: 465 m (1525 ft)
Maximum elevation: 2365 m (7760 ft)
Maps: Gem Trek 1:100,000 Banff & Mt. Assiniboine and NTS 1:50,000 Spray Lakes Reservoir 82 J/14
Trailhead: Km 15.0 of *Palliser Pass* trail (see p. 76).

0.0 — Sign (elevation 1900 m). Turn southeast (left); Palliser Pass straight ahead. Climb steeply.

3.5 — Burstall Pass (2365 m) and Banff National Park boundary. Trail continues east in Alberta's Kananaskis Country recreation area, descending to a parking area on the Smith-Dorrien/Spray Trail (road) in 7.5 km.

This trail from the upper valley of the Spray River to the lofty heights of Burstall Pass is most often used by backpackers, usually in the opposite direction to this description.

Leman Lake and Spray Pass are visible from Burstall Pass, and are approached more directly via it than by means of the *Palliser Pass* trail. (This way does, however, entail considerably more elevation gain and loss.)

Keep in mind that snow lingers long into summer around the top of this pass.

Northwest from Burstall Pass with Mt. Assiniboine in distance (third peak from left).

Owl Lake

Distance: 5.2 km (3.2 mi) — *Bryant Creek* trail to south end of Owl Lake
Day hike: 1.5—2 hours one way
Elevation loss: 30 m (100 ft)
Elevation gain: 150 m (490 ft)
Maximum elevation: 1900 m (6230 ft)
Maps: Gem Trek 1:100,000 Banff & Mt. Assiniboine and NTS 1:50,000 Mount Assiniboine 82 J/13
Trailhead: Km 11.7 of *Bryant Creek* trail (see p. 74).

0.0 — Sign (elevation 1770 m). Descend to the southwest.
0.3 — Turn right; ford for horse parties straight ahead.
0.5 — Cross footbridge (1750 m) over Bryant Creek. Turn left.
0.7 — Turn right where rejoin trail from horse ford. Begin steady climb.
3.2 — High point (1900 m).
3.7 — Turn right to travel along west shore; trail to left leads to north end of Owl Lake in 100 metres (straight ahead dead-ends on a peninsula).
5.2 — South end of Owl Lake (1890 m).

Owl Lake is an attractive destination off the *Bryant Creek* trail, making for an enjoyable trip even if none of its namesakes are seen. The approach climbs steadily through forest; the side trail that leads to the lake at the first view ends at a logjam and not much of a panorama.

If the water level is high enough, the two small lakes at the northeast end of Owl Lake are incorporated into the larger body of water.

By far the best part of visiting Owl Lake is venturing onto the section of trail along the west shore, from which there are fine vistas of Mt. Byng and its rugged outliers. This west side trail also passes beneath the steep grey cliffs of Marvel Peak, down which run a number of avalanche gullies (slides of snow and broken trees can block the way).

Trail along west shore of Owl Lake; Mt. Byng to south.

Marvel Pass

Distance: 9.1 km (5.6 mi) — South end of Owl Lake to south end of *Wonder Pass* trail and west end of *Marvel Lake* trail
Extension to day hike: 3—4 hours one way
Elevation gain: 460 m (1510 ft)
Elevation loss: 400 m (1310 ft)
Maximum elevation: 2190 m (7180 ft)
Maps: Gem Trek 1:100,000 Banff & Mt. Assiniboine and NTS 1:50,000 Mount Assiniboine 82 J/13
Trailhead: South end of Owl Lake at km 5.2 of *Owl Lake* trail.

0.0 — South end of Owl Lake (elevation 1890 m). Travel upsteam through meadows in valley on west side of Owl Creek.

1.5 — South end of meadows; faint trail leads up to the west. Climb steeply.

3.5 — Marvel Pass (2190 m). To continue toward Marvel Lake, descend to small unnamed lake west of pass, then bear northwest (do not head down Aurora Creek) toward long, narrow lakes at head of Marvel Creek. Pick up trail that descends partway down drainage through meadows before cutting into forest and descending switchbacks.

8.1 — West end of Marvel Lake (1790 m). Cross channels of outlet stream from Gloria and Terrapin lakes. Climb steeply.

9.1 — South end (1950 m) of *Wonder Pass* trail and west end of *Marvel Lake* trail.

This is a trip that requires a good sense of direction and well-developed navigation and routefinding skills. The first part, to near an old outfitter's camp at the end of the meadows southeast of Owl Lake, is straightforward.

However, it may be necessary to cast about to pick up the trail toward the pass, which starts faintly up to the right (not along the creek). Climb steeply toward a rocky rib of a subsidiary to Marvel Peak, then contour to the larch-surrounded pass.

Glacier lilies grace the saddle with yellow in early summer. Just below Marvel Pass is a small unnamed lake that has the remains of an abandoned cabin beside its shore.

If decide to head to Marvel Lake, be careful not to follow the faint path that leads southwest down Aurora Creek. Rather, head northwest to a chain of shallow lakes. Then some bushwhacking might ensue, but eventually pick up a faint trail heading north down the drainage of Marvel Creek.

Late-lying snow on this north-facing slope can increase the difficulties in figuring out the route, besides impeding progress. The way becomes clearer on switchbacks in old-growth forest. These lead to multiple creek crossings below Lake Gloria and Lake Terrapin, downstream from a waterfall.

The trail then climbs steeply to the end of the *Marvel Lake* trail, which point is also the start of the *Wonder Pass* trail.

Marvel Lake

Distance: 6.6 km (4.1 mi) — *Bryant Creek* trail to above west end of Marvel Lake
Day hike/backpack: 2—2.5 hours one way
Elevation gain: 155 m (510 ft)
Maximum elevation: 1950 m (6395 ft)
Maps: Gem Trek 1:100,000 Banff & Mt. Assiniboine and NTS 1:50,000 Mount Assiniboine 82 J/13
Trailhead: Km 12.7 of *Bryant Creek* trail (see p. 74).

0.0 — Sign (elevation 1795 m). Climb gradually to west.

0.6 — Backcountry campground.

1.6 — Northeast corner of Marvel Lake. Keep right; path to left leads to outlet in 300 metres.

2.1 — Keep left; connector to right leads to *Bryant Creek* trail in 1.1 km. Begin steady traversing climb above north end of Marvel Lake.

6.6 — End of *Marvel Lake* trail (1950 m) above west end of lake. *Wonder Pass* trail up to right; *Marvel Pass* trail down to left.

The most direct approach to Marvel Lake from the *Bryant Creek* trail turns off at km 12.7 to pass by a backcountry campground before arriving at the northeast corner of the lake. A short spur trail runs south to the outlet into Marvel Creek, where large cutthroat trout shelter under the logjam (fishing prohibited here, and below on Marvel Creek to its confluence with Bryant Creek).

The main trail heads up through forest to join the alternate route from the northeast, then veers west to begin a long gradually ascending course high above the lake. The sunny south-facing slopes support a wide array of wildflowers, including double bladderpod with its yellow blossoms, distinctive basal leaves, and deep taproot.

Other species that might be in bloom are stonecrop, alumroot, scorpionweed, and—surprising in this dry setting—sparrow's-egg lady's slipper (an orchid). Foraging on the vegetation are mammals such as pikas and least chipmunks.

The high traverse grants expansive views, including of the fair-sized island in the lake near its east end and of the northern aspects of Marvel Peak and its outliers across the lake.

Double bladderpod.

Wonder Pass

Distance: 3.3 km (2.0 mi) — West end of *Marvel Lake* trail (or north end of *Marvel Pass* trail) to Wonder Pass
Day hike/backpack: 1.5—2 hours one way
Elevation gain: 445 m (1460 ft)
Maximum elevation: 2395 m (7855 ft)
Maps: Gem Trek 1:100,000 Banff & Mt. Assiniboine and NTS 1:50,000 Mount Assiniboine 82 J/13
Trailhead: West end of *Marvel Lake* trail at km 6.6, or north end of *Marvel Pass* trail at km 9.1 (see p. 83).

0.0 — Sign (elevation 1950 m). Turn up to north; *Marvel Pass* trail down to south. Climb steep switchbacks.

2.6 — Keep straight; to right is a side trail to a viewpoint.

3.3 — Wonder Pass (2395 m) and Alberta/British Columbia boundary. Trail continues north into B.C.'s Mount Assiniboine Provincial Park.

The ascent of Wonder Pass from the south climbs via a series of well-designed switchbacks. At the culmination of the steady haul up, this high saddle grants views southwest to the glaciated summits of Mt. Gloria and Eon Mountain. To the south rise the jagged crests of Aurora Mountain, Mt. Alcantara, and the unnamed peak between them.

The viewpoint accessible via a side trail below the pass affords the best views of Lake Gloria and Marvel Lake, named by A.O. Wheeler for their magnificent colours. Wonder Pass is the southeastern doorstep of Mount Assiniboine Provincial Park.

This trail is mostly taken in the opposite direction, by backpackers exiting from Lake Magog having entered on the lower approach over Assiniboine Pass via the *Bryant Creek* trail.

South from Wonder Pass.

Allenby Pass

Distance: 5.8 km (3.6 mi) — *Bryant Creek* trail to Allenby Pass
Day hike/backpack: 2—2.5 hours one way
Elevation gain: 535 m (1755 ft)
Maximum elevation: 2435 m (7985 ft)
Maps: Gem Trek 1:100,000 Banff & Mt. Assiniboine and NTS 1:50,000 Mount Assiniboine 82 J/13
Trailhead: Km 17.7 of *Bryant Creek* trail (see p. 74).

0.0 — Keep right (elevation 1900 m); to left leads toward Assiniboine Pass.
1.9 — Keep straight (2070 m); *Og Pass* trail to left.
3.6 — Cross intermittent stream.
4.1 — Switchback up through stand of subalpine larch, then traverse northwest.
5.8 — Allenby Pass (2435 m). *Brewster Creek* trail descends to north.

The route to Allenby Pass from the south starts with steep switchbacks to climb out of the valley of Bryant Creek. The going is more gentle after the junction with the *Og Pass* trail. Work up Allenby Creek, with the steep slabs of Mt. Allenby soaring above.

The final approach makes a hard right turn to switchback up through an extensive stand of subalpine larch, then runs virtually on a contour the rest of the way to the pass.

A botanical highlight of the scree slopes traversed on the last stretch is the presence of round clusters of silver rockcress. This species is also known as alpine smelowskia after the first part of its Latin name, *Smelowskia calycina.*

The *Brewster Creek* trail descends north from Allenby Pass; it's possible to hike all the way to Banff townsite as done almost a century ago.

Allenby Pass **trail south of the pass.**

Og Pass

Distance: 5.6 km (3.4 mi) — *Allenby Pass* trail to Og Pass
Day hike/backpack: 1.5—2 hours one way
Elevation gain: 230 m (755 ft)
Maximum elevation: 2300 m (7545 ft)
Maps: Gem Trek 1:100,000 Banff & Mt. Assiniboine and NTS 1:50,000 Mount Assiniboine 82 J/13
Trailhead: Km 1.9 of *Allenby Pass* trail.

0.0 — Trail sign (elevation 2070 m). Head west on wide trail contouring along slope.

2.5 — Turn northwest and begin ascent on narrower trail.

5.6 — Og Pass (2300 m) and Alberta/British Columbia boundary. Trail continues west into B.C.'s Mount Assiniboine Provincial Park.

Og Pass provides yet another approach into Mount Assiniboine Provincial Park from Bryant Creek, although this route is used even less than that over Wonder Pass. The high traverse west toward Cave Mountain from the *Allenby Pass* trail gives an outstanding perspective of Mt. Assiniboine rising above Assiniboine Pass.

The trail then swings northwest and commences the steep ascent to Og Pass, travelling beside the steep east wall of Cave Mountain to a tiny lake that is the source of Bryant Creek.

Creek beside Og Pass trail.

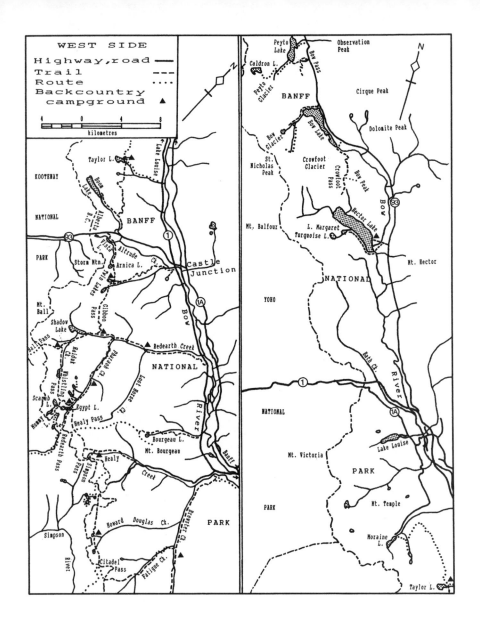

West Side

Bourgeau Lake from knoll east of Harvey Pass.

Bourgeau Lake

Distance: 7.5 km (4.7 mi) — Trans-Canada Highway to Bourgeau Lake
Day hike: 2.5—3 hours one way
Elevation gain: 710 m (2330 ft)
Maximum elevation: 2155 m (7070 ft)
Maps: Gem Trek 1:100,000 Banff & Mt. Assiniboine and NTS 1:50,000 Banff 82-O/4
Trailhead: Parking area on west side of eastbound lanes of Trans-Canada Highway, 0.5 km (0.3 mi) south of bridge over Wolverine Creek. This parking area is accessible from the westbound lanes by using the left turn lane 2.8 km (1.7 mi) north of Sunshine interchange (stop before crossing the eastbound lanes).

0.0 — Trailhead kiosk (elevation 1445 m). Head west into forest and begin steady climb.
2.5 — Cross avalanche chute.
3.7 — Cross footbridge over tributary of Wolverine Creek flowing from south.
5.5 — Use rock cribs to cross Wolverine Creek below waterfall. Begin steep climb up switchbacks.
6.8 — Trail levels out in meadows of lake basin.
7.5 — Northeast corner of Bourgeau Lake (2155 m).

Heading up south of the gorge of Wolverine Creek, this trail passes through a zone of Douglas-fir before crossing a slide path that gives views east to the toothy Sawback Range (named by Sir James Hector in 1858). To the northwest is an unnamed outlier of Mt. Brett, on whose slanting ledges can be observed mountain goats and bighorn sheep.

The big boulders at the northeast corner of Bourgeau Lake are often frequented by golden-mantled ground squirrels and least chipmunks. The profuse flora that can be seen includes western anemone, mountain sorrel, and glacier lily.

Although the ease of access of this trail may make it tempting when want to get up high early in the hiking season, keep in mind that its elevation and its sheltered situation result in deep snow lingering well into summer.

The name of the lake and of the adjacent mountain honour Eugene Bourgeau, the popular French-born botanist of the 1857-1859 Palliser Expedition.

Sawback Range from *Bourgeau Lake* trail.

Harvey Pass

Distance: 2.4 km (1.5 mi) — Bourgeau Lake to Harvey Pass
Extension to day hike: 1 hour one way
Elevation gain: 295 m (970 ft)
Maximum elevation: 2450 m (8040 ft)
Maps: Gem Trek 1:100,000 Banff & Mt. Assiniboine and NTS 1:50,000 Banff 82-O/4
Trailhead: Km 7.5 of *Bourgeau Lake* trail.

0.0 — Northeast corner of Bourgeau Lake (elevation 2155 m). Take narrow path through forest to north of lake, then climb north (preferably staying east of drainage) on rocky slopes.

1.2 — Level out after notch; travel along north shore of shallow lake and turn south above headwall. Climb steadily.

2.2 — Harvey Lake. Take path along east shore.

2.4 — South end of Harvey Pass (2450 m).

A tougher still trail goes on from the end of the *Bourgeau Lake* trail to Harvey Pass. En route is a small lake, near which may be found the bright pink blossoms of moss campion. This ground-hugging wildflower with its pincushion-like growth form is an indicator species of the alpine zone, and a welcome sign of having reached the high country.

Veering left after the small lake, the trail climbs along the top of a sloping headwall to reach Harvey Lake set in the gap of Harvey Pass. This small body of water is often icebound into August and is subject to avalanches. The south end of the pass grants superlative views, including of Mt. Assiniboine with its steep ridges soaring skyward on the horizon.

It's an easy scramble up the knoll east of Harvey Pass. If venture carefully to the edge, Bourgeau Lake is revealed nestled in the cirque far below. A more ambitious off-trail option is to have a go at getting up Mt. Bourgeau via the west ridge...not that it's technical, but it involves climbing another 480 metres vertical to reach the summit at 2931 m (9615 ft).

Walking on the coarse shale near the top makes a jingling sound, like Chinese bells. The abrupt east face of the mountain, a landmark from the Bow Valley, is likely to be overhung by a huge cornice [see photo p. 26], so don't get toward the edge. Telecommunications gear on Mt. Bourgeau spoils the wilderness sense, but there are still outstanding panoramas from the peak. Pioneer explorers J.J. McArthur and Tom Wilson made the first recorded ascent in 1890.

An interesting option for cross-country travel enthusiasts is to venture over the open ridges west of Harvey Pass. It's possible to connect with Healy Pass. (See the author's *Ridgewalks in the Canadian Rockies*, Luminous Compositions, 2001.) There is a bit of a trail at first, which soon fades out, but well-defined animal paths occur on the ridgecrests. This is most enjoyable rambling, with wide open views to the south over the Sunshine Meadows and to the north over the far less often seen meadows at the head of Lost Horse Creek. This stream was named because, indeed, a horse was lost in its valley by outfitter Pat Brewster in the 1920s.

Citadel Pass

Distance: 9.0 km (5.6 mi) — Sunshine downhill ski area to Citadel Pass
Day hike/backpack: 2—2.5 hours one way
Elevation gain: 315 m (1035 ft)
Elevation loss: 150 m (490 ft)
Maximum elevation: 2360 m (7740 ft)
Maps: Gem Trek 1:100,000 Banff & Mt. Assiniboine and NTS 1:50,000 Banff 82-O/4
Trailhead: Take the 9.0 km (5.6 mi) paved road from the Sunshine interchange on the Trans-Canada Highway, which is 9.0 km (5.6 mi) west of the Norquay interchange near Banff townsite. The trailhead is at the Sunshine downhill ski area complex at the end of the 6.5 km (4.0 mi) gated access road that starts at the southwest corner of parking area. The trailhead is most easily reached on the shuttle bus operated by White Mountain Tours, phone (403) 678-4099. The access road can be hiked (boring); it is not open to mountain bikes.

0.0 — Parks Canada cabin (elevation 2195 m) just south of and above the ski area complex. Head left at junction just south of cabin and begin steady ascent.

1.1 — Keep left (2300 m); right leads to Rock Isle Lake.

3.9 — Low point (2250 m) in valley north of Quartz Ridge.

5.0 — Quartz Ridge (2385 m). Descend south on less well-maintained trail.

5.6 — Howard Douglas Lake (2285 m) and backcountry campground. Trail continues southeast after crossing outlet stream.

9.0 — Citadel Pass (2360 m) and Alberta/British Columbia boundary. Main trail continues south into Mount Assiniboine Provincial Park, reaching Magog Lake in 19.7 km (12.2 mi) from the pass; intermittent trail to east leads to Fatigue Pass and southwest end of *Fatigue Creek* trail in 2.5 km.

Mt. Assiniboine from *Citadel Pass* trail at Quartz Ridge.

Howard Douglas Lake and Citadel Peak (with Citadel Pass to its left) from Quartz Ridge.

The Sunshine Meadows, renowned for their open expanses and floral displays, form the attractive surroundings on the hike to Citadel Pass. In good weather, this outing is one of the most scenic in the Canadian Rockies. The high rolling plateau gives the sensation of being able to continue almost forever.

There is a jog in the Alberta/British Columbia boundary that sees a brief visit to B.C. not far from the trailhead (Rock Isle and the other nearby lakes are in Mount Assiniboine Provincial Park). The trail goes back into Banff National Park within a kilometre or so, then dips into a wide shallow bowl before climbing a few switchbacks to the low point on Quartz Ridge.

Here is the first view of Howard Douglas Lake, named after the park's second superintendent. (It may be incorrectly marked as Sundown Lake on some maps.) Drop down 100 metres vertical on less well-established trail {avoid creating further braids} to reach the shore in 600 metres. There is a backcountry campground on the north side of the lake, before the outlet stream: it can serve as a base for hikes in the area.

To continue to Citadel Pass, cross the outlet stream on strategically placed rocks and follow a narrow defile upward before rising gently to the southeast below Citadel Peak. Conditions on the tundra-like terrain can be balmy on a fine day, or the weather can be windy and chilly even in mid-summer.

Whatever the conditions, it's possible to savour the variety of flora that thrives here. Glacier lilies can be seen early in the season; later the species in bloom include alpine speedwell, with small blue flowers, and moss campion, whose bright pink blossoms rise just above the tight island of emerald green leaves.

Simpson Pass

Distance: 7.6 km (4.7 mi) — Sunshine downhill ski area to *Egypt Lake via Healy Pass* trail via Simpson Pass
Day hike/backpack: 2—2.5 hours one way
Elevation gain: 250 m (820 ft)
Elevation loss: 225 m (740 ft)
Maximum elevation: 2355 m (7725 ft)
Maps: Gem Trek 1:100,000 Banff & Mt. Assiniboine and NTS 1:50,000 Banff 82-O/4
Trailhead: As for *Citadel Pass* trail (see p. 92).

0.0 — Sign (elevation 2195 m) west of upper gondola terminal. Take trail, here called "Meadow Park," up to northwest.

1.7 — Keep straight; "Twin Cairns" trail leads south to Rock Isle Lake in Mount Assiniboine Provincial Park, B.C., with connector to Standish Ridge.

1.9 — High point (2355 m) on Wawa Ridge. Descend to west, then drop north to contour below cliffs before descending to southwest.

5.6 — Simpson Pass (2130 m) and Alberta/British Columbia boundary. Keep straight, climbing to west for a short distance. (Trail north from pass connects in 1.3 km with *Egypt Lake via Healy Pass* trail at km 5.9.)

6.0 — Keep straight; to left is 3.2 km trail to Eohippus Lake in Mount Assiniboine Provincial Park. Level out in meadows with numerous small lakes.

7.6 — Intersection (2220 m) with *Egypt Lake via Healy Pass* trail at km 7.7. Keep straight for Healy Pass; right leads down Healy Creek.

Simpson Pass is a low saddle in a small meadow rimmed by subalpine larch. Its name and that of the river flowing south from it commemorate Sir George Simpson, Governor of the Hudson's Bay Company in 1841 when he used the pass as an exit from the Bow Valley in the course of a round-the-world trip.

There are two ways to join the *Egypt Lake via Healy Pass* trail from Simpson Pass: head north directly down to Healy Creek, or keep going west if wish to attain Healy Pass. The latter route takes a tarn-filled bench below the Monarch Ramparts.

Northwest from near where *Simpson Pass* trail crosses Wawa Ridge; Pharaoh Peaks (left) and Mt. Ball (left of centre).

Egypt Lake via Healy Pass

Distance: 12.5 km (7.8 mi) — Sunshine downhill ski area parking area to Egypt Lake backcountry campground
Day hike/backpack: 3.5—4 hours one way
Elevation gain: 695 m (2280 ft)
Elevation loss: 375 m (1230 ft)
Maximum elevation: 2330 m (7640 ft)
Maps: Gem Trek 1:100,000 Banff & Mt. Assiniboine and NTS 1:50,000 Banff 82-O/4
Trailhead: Take the 9.0 km (5.6 mi) paved road from the Sunshine interchange on the Trans-Canada Highway, which is 9.0 km (5.6 mi) west of the Norquay interchange near Banff townsite. The trailhead is behind (west of) the lower gondola terminal [don't take the access road from the southwest corner of parking area].

0.0 — Trailhead kiosk behind lower gondola terminal (elevation 1675 m). Head west up wide track.

0.8 — Turn right off wide track at sign (1740 m). Descend gradually.

1.0 — Cross footbridge (1710 m) and begin steady climb.

3.1 — Cross Healy Creek on footbridge.

5.5 — Backcountry campground.

5.9 — Keep right; trail to left crosses Healy Creek on footbridge and climbs to Simpson Pass in 1.3 km. Begin to climb more steeply.

7.7 — Cross footbridge (2220 m) and keep right; *Simpson Pass* trail to left. Climb through upper subalpine and alpine meadows.

9.2 — Healy Pass (2330 m). To continue to Egypt Lake, veer north for 50 metres before descending to northwest.

12.3 — Keep straight (1985 m); warden cabin to right and *Redearth Pass* trail to left. Cross Pharaoh Creek on footbridge and climb to terrace.

12.5 — Egypt Lake backcountry campground and trail shelter (1995 m). Egypt Lake itself is 0.9 km away via the *Whistling Pass* trail (see p. 98).

The trail to Egypt Lake via Healy Pass stays mostly in forest as it works up the valley of Healy Creek, although it does cross several wide slide paths off cliffs to the northwest after the footbridge at km 3.1.

Soon after the backcountry campground at km 5.5, pass the junction with the shortest approach to Simpson Pass from this direction. A steep stretch follows before arriving at glorious open meadows interspersed with subalpine larch. Now reap the benefits of steadily improving views, and—if it's early summer—a solid yellow ground cover of glacier lilies.

The vistas to the south encompass the numerous small lakes dotting the meadows toward Simpson Pass, the rolling terrain of the Sunshine Meadows, and in the distance the "Matterhorn of the Canadian Rockies," Mt. Assiniboine. The often windy crest of Healy Pass gives the first sight of Egypt and Scarab lakes, plus a horizon full of hitherto hidden peaks—including uniquely shaped Mt. Hector near Lake Louise, some 60 km to the northwest.

An off-trail trip can be made from Healy Pass along the crest of (cont. p. 96) (cont. from p. 95) the Monarch Ramparts, although contrary to the level and linear appearance from below this route is undulating and meandering. Despite often blustery conditions (of which the large cornice that forms on the leeward side is evidence), the ridge supports a variety of wildflowers. An intriguing example of the flora here is alpine lousewort, which has bright purple blossoms.

An off-trail excursion can also be made north from Healy Pass. Head across meadows, then pick up a path leading up the ridge to a large cairn at the summit of a small peak. This feature—elevation approximately 2545 m (8350 ft)—gives views into the remote valley of Lost Horse Creek, and can be visited as part of a cross-country jaunt to or from Bourgeau Lake (see *Harvey Pass* trail description, p. 91).

The distance to Egypt Lake via this approach and the elevation loss from the pass combine to usually make it the destination of an overnight trip rather than a day hike. There is a backcountry campground near the lake, as well as a park-operated trail shelter.

The Egypt Lake area with its many hiking options is justifiably popular, thus is not usually a place to find solitude. The names of Egypt Lake and of several nearby features were bestowed by the Topographical Survey in the early 1900s.

Backpacker at Healy Pass, with Pharaoh Peaks and Mt. Ball on left.

Redearth Pass

Distance: 2.8 km (1.7 mi) — *Egypt Lake via Healy Pass* trail to Redearth Pass
Day hike/backpack: 30—45 minutes one way
Elevation gain: 95 m (310 ft)
Maximum elevation: 2080 m (6820 ft)
Maps: Gem Trek 1:100,000 Banff & Mt. Assiniboine and NTS 1:50,000 Banff 82-O/4
Trailhead: Km 12.3 of *Egypt Lake via Healy Pass* trail (see p. 95).

0.0 — Junction (elevation 1985 m). Head south, upstream along east bank of Pharaoh Creek.

2.3 — Keep straight; right leads to Natalko Lake, Kootenay National Park, British Columbia, in gradual 1.7 km.

2.8 — Redearth Pass (2080 m) and Alberta/British Columbia boundary. Trail continues to south (vague in places), down East Verdant Creek in Kootenay National Park and to Highway 93 South in 18.2 km.

This relaxing amble provides for a brief excursion from Egypt Lake. Following the course of Pharaoh Creek, travel through meadows in a narrow valley to reach Redearth Pass on the Alberta/B.C. boundary. Given that the pass is at the divide between Pharaoh and East Verdant creeks, and nowhere near Redearth Creek, the name is curious.

When travelling from the pass toward Egypt Lake there is a good view of the southernmost Pharaoh Peak, which looks remarkably like the summit block of Mt. Everest as seen from the west.

A trail continues south from Redearth Pass into Kootenay National Park, down East Verdant Creek to Verdant Creek and up through the gap of Honeymoon Pass in Hawk Ridge before descending to Vermilion Crossing.

A shorter jaunt starting at km 2.3 leads to Natalko (or Talc) Lake via a wide, well-graded trail. This track was part of the route via Pharaoh and Redearth creeks that was once used to haul talc out to the Bow Valley. The last shipments were made from December, 1943, to March, 1944, when—under the War Measures Act—7.5 tons were taken for military purposes. There are signs at the lake of the now completely abandoned mine, whose deposits were originally staked by Bill Peyto in 1917 (before the area became part of Kootenay National Park).

An option from Natalko Lake is to head up the draw to the northwest and drop down to Mummy Lake. For the truly energetic, it is possible to scramble to the summit of the small conical peak north of Natalko Lake. This feature, whose summit is at an elevation of 2505 m (8215 ft), gives a dramatic view of Egypt Lake if carefully descend a short distance from the top.

Whistling Pass

Distance: 3.3 km (2.0 mi) — Egypt Lake backcountry campground to Whistling Pass
Day hike/backpack: 1—1.5 hour(s) one way
Elevation gain: 300 m (985 ft)
Maximum elevation: 2295 m (7530 ft)
Maps: Gem Trek 1:100,000 Banff & Mt. Assiniboine and NTS 1:50,000 Banff 82-O/4
Trailhead: Egypt Lake backcountry campground (see p. 95).

0.0 — Backcountry campground (elevation 1995 m). Head southwest.
0.5 — Keep right; to left leads to Egypt Lake in 400 metres. Begin steep climb.
1.9 — Keep right (2225 m); *Mummy Lake* trail to left. Steady ascent.
3.3 — Whistling Pass (2295 m). *Haiduk Creek* trail descends to north.

Whistling Pass is a narrow saddle squeezed between the rugged mountains of the continental divide to the west and the Pharaoh Peaks to the east. It is the most appealing of the many attractive spots near Egypt Lake. After toiling up through cliffs and passing the junction for Mummy and Scarab lakes, veer northwest through more open terrain with a smattering of subalpine larches.

As climbing the last incline to the pass, a loud whistle might be heard. This is the far-carrying alarm call of a hoary marmot, a high country inhabitant whose French name *siffleur* means "whistler."

Whistling Pass grants views of the heavily glaciated summit of Mt. Ball and of Haiduk Lake below. The *Haiduk Creek* trail (see p. 101) leads down to the lake.

Keen scramblers can ascend from the pass to the southernmost and highest of the Pharaoh Peaks. The summit—elevation 2712 m (8895 ft)—allows an unusual airy perspective upon Egypt Lake. A rapid descent can be made to the *Whistling Pass* trail, angling southwest toward the centre of Scarab Lake to bypass cliffs.

Hoary marmot adult and young.

Mummy Lake

Distance: 1.7 km (1.1 mi) — *Whistling Pass* trail to Mummy Lake
Day hike: 30—45 minutes one way
Elevation loss: 105 m (345 ft)
Elevation gain: 130 m (425 ft)
Maximum elevation: 2270 m (7445 ft)
Maps: Gem Trek 1:100,000 Banff & Mt. Assiniboine and NTS 1:50,000 Banff 82-O/4
Trailhead: Km 1.9 of *Whistling Pass* trail.

0.0 — Sign (elevation 2225 m). Keep left; right leads to Whistling Pass. Descend gradually.
0.6 — East end of Scarab Lake (2140 m). Cross outlet stream and climb to southeast (following up drainage to north end of Mummy Lake requires steep scrambling).
1.5 — High point (2270 m). Descend to west.
1.7 — East shore of Mummy Lake (2250 m).

This short side trail leads to two lakes above Egypt Lake. First descend from the *Whistling Pass* trail to Scarab Lake and cross its outlet, which feeds the waterfall on the cliffs above the west side of Egypt Lake.

Then head up a gully and curve around a knoll to arrive at about midway along the east shore of Mummy Lake. It's possible to go around this long, narrow body of water. The park and provincial boundary lies just beyond its south tip; a gap there gives views over Verdant Creek to Hawk Ridge in Kootenay National Park.

It's also feasible to scramble east to Natalko Lake from Mummy Lake: see the *Redearth Pass* trail description (p. 97).

The author at Mummy Lake, with the Pharaoh Peaks to north.

Pharaoh Creek

Distance: 8.7 km (5.4 mi) — Egypt Lake backcountry campground to west end of *Redearth Creek* trail
Day hike/backpack: 2.5—3 hours one way
Elevation loss: 260 m (855 ft)
Maximum elevation: 1995 m (6545 ft)
Maps: Gem Trek 1:100,000 Banff & Mt. Assiniboine and NTS 1:50,000 Banff 82-O/4
Trailhead: Egypt Lake backcountry campground (see p. 95).

0.0 — Backcountry campground (elevation 1995 m). Head north, keeping on west side of Pharaoh Creek.
0.5 — Keep straight (1980 m); to left is *Pharaoh Lake* trail.
0.9 — Cross footbridge to east side of Pharaoh Creek.
3.9 — Cross side stream, usually by stepping across on rocks.
4.3 — Backcountry campground.
4.5 — Cross footbridge to west side of Pharaoh Creek.
5.0 — Cross footbridge to east side of Pharaoh Creek.
5.7 — Cross to west side of Pharaoh Creek on the first of five footbridges in next 3 km.
8.7 — Fifth and final footbridge over Pharaoh Creek, and warden cabin (1735 m). *Redearth Creek* trail continues ahead via footbridge over Redearth Creek.

The trail along Pharaoh Creek is used mainly as an alternate to the *Egypt Lake via Healy Pass* trail to exit or enter the Egypt Lake area.

It is straightforward to the point of being mundane. There is a backcountry campground about midway. Some variety is provided by a series of footbridges before joining the *Redearth Creek* trail.

Pharaoh Lake

Distance: 1.3 km (0.8 mi) — *Pharaoh Creek* trail to Pharaoh Lake
Day hike: 30—45 minutes one way
Elevation gain: 145 m (475 ft)
Maximum elevation: 2125 m (6970 ft)
Maps: Gem Trek 1:100,000 Banff & Mt. Assiniboine and NTS 1:50,000 Banff 82-O/4
Trailhead: Km 0.5 of *Pharaoh Creek* trail.

0.0 — Sign (elevation 1980 m). Head steeply up to the west.
1.3 — Southeast corner of Pharaoh Lake (2125 m).

This short but steep outing leads to the largest of a series of three bodies of water tucked at the eastern base of the Pharaoh Peaks. Black Rock Lake is 1.1 km further; determined hikers can push on to tiny Sphinx Lake in an additional 1.6 km.

Haiduk Creek

Distance: 9.7 km (6.0 mi) — Whistling Pass to west end of *Shadow Lake* trail
Day hike/backpack: 3—3.5 hours one way
Elevation loss: 455 m (1490 ft)
Maximum elevation: 2295 m (7530 ft)
Maps: Gem Trek 1:100,000 Banff & Mt. Assiniboine and NTS 1:50,000 Banff 82-O/4
Trailhead: End of *Whistling Pass* trail from Egypt Lake (see p. 98)

0.0 — Whistling Pass (elevation 2295 m). Descend to the north.
1.7 — South end of Haiduk Lake; follow along east shore.
2.8 — Cross Haiduk Creek.
4.8 — Veer west away from Haiduk Creek.
5.4 — Cross footbridge and keep right (1920 m); backcountry campground and *Ball Pass* trail to left. Travel downstream, skirting boggy areas.
9.6 — Cross footbridge at outlet of Shadow lake.
9.7 — East end of Shadow Lake (1840 m) and west end of *Shadow Lake* trail.

Descending from Whistling Pass, this trail drops steeply to Haiduk Lake. Surveyor and mountaineer A.O. Wheeler wrote that he named this remote body of water from the Polish word meaning "lively" or "vigorous," for when he first saw it "the sun, like diamonds, [was] sparkling on its wind-blown ripples."

From this pristine lake the trail follows the valley of Haiduk Creek down toward the east end of Shadow Lake. En route pass the Ball Pass junction, site of a backcountry campground where the author and four other backpackers once enjoyed the sight of an adult bald eagle soaring overhead.

**Haiduk Peak from
Haiduk Lake.**

Ball Pass

Distance: 2.7 km (1.7 mi) — *Haiduk Creek* trail to Ball Pass
Day hike/backpack: 1—1.5 hour(s) one way
Elevation gain: 290 m (950 ft)
Maximum elevation: 2210 m (7250 ft)
Maps: Gem Trek 1:100,000 Banff & Mt. Assiniboine and NTS 1:50,000 Banff 82-O/4
Trailhead: Km 5.4 of *Haiduk Creek* trail (see p. 101); accessible via the *Whistling Pass* trail (see p. 98) and the *Shadow Lake* trail (see p. 104).

0.0 — Sign (elevation 1920 m). Head west, climbing steadily.
2.1 — Begin steep ascent over rocky slope.
2.7 — Ball Pass (2210 m) and Alberta/British Columbia boundary. Trail continues south, descending the Hawk Creek trail in Kootenay National Park to Highway 93 South in a further 9.7 km.

This jaunt to the continental divide off the *Haiduk Creek* trail is recommended, especially for the vistas it gives of the impressive glaciers and icefalls on the southern aspect of Mt. Ball. At 3307 m (10,847 ft), the summit of this towering peak is the highest point on the interprovincial boundary between Mt. Assiniboine and the Ten Peaks southwest of Moraine Lake.

The east end of Shadow Lake is also visible from Ball Pass. The trail continues south, dropping steeply to the Banff—Windermere Parkway.

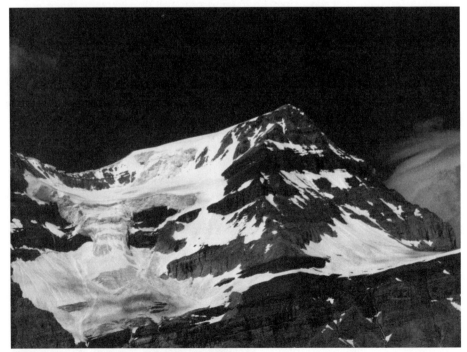

Glaciated summit of Mt. Ball from Ball Pass.

Redearth Creek

Distance: 11.1 km (6.9 mi) — Trans-Canada Highway to end of former fire road
Day hike/backpack: 3—3.5 hours one way
Elevation gain: 335 m (1100 ft)
Maximum elevation: 1735 m (5690 ft)
Maps: Gem Trek 1:100,000 Banff & Mt. Assiniboine and NTS 1:50,000 Banff 82-O/4
Trailhead: Redearth Creek parking area on west side of Trans-Canada Highway, 20.0 km (12.4 mi) northwest of Mt. Norquay interchange near Banff townsite and 10.5 km (6.5 mi) southeast of Castle Junction.

0.0 — Trailhead kiosk (elevation 1400 m). Climb through gate in wildlife fencing and head up steep, narrow trail.
0.3 — Keep right where join former fire road. Moderate climb.
7.0 — Cross footbridge over Lost Horse Creek.
7.2 — Cross footbridge over Redearth Creek. Backcountry campground.
10.8 — Keep straight; *Shadow Lake* trail to right.
11.1 — Footbridge (1735 m) over Redearth Creek and warden cabin; *Pharaoh Creek* trail to south.

This former fire road serves as the approach to a number of interesting hikes, such as to Shadow Lake, Ball Pass, Whistling Pass, Gibbon Pass, and Twin Lakes. In conjunction with the *Pharaoh Creek* trail, it also gives access to the Egypt Lake area via a longer but lower and gentler route than that over Healy Pass.

The old road is usually a rather uneventful slog, enlivened by views of the steep south face of Copper Mountain and, to the southeast, the impressive western aspect of the summit block of Pilot Mountain.

Mountain biking is permitted on this trail, but not on the *Pharaoh Creek* or *Shadow Lake* trails that continue beyond it.

Dew-bedecked harebell.

Shadow Lake

Distance: 3.5 km (2.2 mi) — *Redearth Creek* trail to Shadow Lake
Day hike/backpack: 1—1.5 hour(s) one way
Elevation gain: 105 m (345 ft)
Maximum elevation: 1840 m (6035 ft)
Maps: Gem Trek 1:100,000 Banff & Mt. Assiniboine and NTS 1:50,000 Banff 82-O/4
Trailhead: Km 10.8 of *Redearth Creek* trail (see p. 103).

0.0 — Sign (elevation 1735 m). Head up west through forest.
2.4 — Outfitter's lodge and cabins.
2.6 — Keep straight (1830 m); backcountry campground and *Gibbon Pass* trail to right.
3.5 — East end of Shadow Lake (1840 m). *Haiduk Creek* trail to Whistling Pass and Egypt Lake, with Ball Pass option, takes footbridge across outlet. (A rough trail goes about 4.5 km along the north side of the lake and to a glacier beneath Mt. Ball.)

This spur off the *Redearth Creek* trail leads to two-kilometre-long Shadow Lake, situated below the impressive east face of Mt. Ball.

En route, pass the backcountry campground at the junction with the *Gibbon Pass* trail, and shortly before the more luxurious accommodation of the Shadow Lake Lodge and Cabins. For rates and information, call (403) 762-0116, fax (403) 760-2866, write P.O. Box 2606, Banff, Alberta, Canada T0L 0C0, or visit the website www.brewsteradventures.com.

**Mt. Ball from east end
of Shadow Lake.**

Gibbon Pass

Distance: 6.0 km (3.7 mi) — *Shadow Lake* trail to *Twin Lakes* trail
Day hike/backpack: 2—2.5 hours one way
Elevation gain: 470 m (1540 ft)
Elevation loss: 245 m (805 ft)
Maximum elevation: 2300 m (7545 ft)
Maps: Gem Trek 1:100,000 Banff & Mt. Assiniboine and NTS 1:50,000 Banff 82-O/4
Trailhead: Km 2.6 of *Shadow Lake* trail.

0.0 — Sign (elevation 1830 m) at backcountry campground. Climb steeply through forest to north.
3.1 — Gibbon Pass (2300 m) in subalpine meadows. Trail to north stays high (rather than dropping to south end of Lower Twin Lake as shown on some maps).
5.8 — Cross outlet stream at north end of Lower Twin Lake.
6.0 — Km 8.0 of *Twin Lakes* trail (2055 m).

This trail goes from near Shadow Lake to the Twin Lakes by way of the pass named for John Murray Gibbon (1875-1952), who was involved in founding the Skyline Trail Hikers in 1933. Gibbon was a public relations agent for the Canadian Pacific Railway. He wrote a history of the CPR, and served as first president of the Canadian Authors Association.

The larch-fringed meadows at Gibbon Pass grant a view to the south of ridges receding in the distance, culminating with the unmistakable summit of Mt. Assiniboine. This view reinforces the connection with Gibbon, since the railway frequently used the image of that famous mountain in advertisements.

The author by cairn at Gibbon Pass.

Twin Lakes

Distance: 8.8 km (5.4 mi) — Parking area at Altrude Creek to Upper Twin Lake
Day hike/backpack: 2.5—3 hours one way
Elevation gain: 540 m (1770 ft)
Maximum elevation: 2090 m (6855 ft)
Maps: Gem Trek 1:100,000 Banff & Mt. Assiniboine, and NTS 1:50,000 Castle Mountain 82-O/5 and Banff 82-O/4
Trailhead: Turn south off lane leading to Trans-Canada Highway at east end of Highway 93 South (if approaching via the Trans-Canada, exit at Castle Junction and take the westbound lane of Highway 93 South to 50 metres west of the stop sign where the exit lane off the eastbound Trans-Canada joins Highway 93 South, then turn south to a stop sign). Cross a cattleguard at the wildlife fencing and travel 200 metres on a narrow, two-way road to the parking area [do not continue to the right on the road].

0.0 — Trailhead kiosk (elevation 1450 m). Head over footbridge on Altrude Creek.
0.1 — Turn right on old road; Copper Lake 600 metres to left.
0.3 — Keep straight (1455 m); *Smith Lake* trail to left.
0.6 — Enter forest on narrow path.
0.9 — Cross footbridge. Climb steadily.
6.4 — Trail levels out in meadows on north side of outlet stream from Twin Lakes: ambiguous in places.
8.0 — Keep right (2055 m); *Gibbon Pass* trail to left—leads to Lower Twin Lake in 200 metres. Moderate climb.
8.8 — Upper Twin Lake (2090 m) and backcountry campground. *Arnica Lake* trail continues to north.

The route to the Twin Lakes from the Trans-Canada Highway is a long, usually mundane climb through forest; the more scenic and slightly shorter approach via the *Arnica Lake* trail might be preferable even though it is steeper.

The route described here is perhaps best used as an exit to the Bow Valley, for example on a backpacking trip started on Highway 93 South. Keep in mind that this choice ends far from other trailheads.

However reached, the Twin Lakes are a worthwhile destination. Lying below the impressive east face of Storm Mountain, they boast larch-embroidered shores and clear, cool depths. The Upper Twin Lake backcountry campground is a good base for venturing to Arnica Lake and Gibbon Pass.

Smith Lake

Distance: 1.3 km (0.8 mi) — *Twin Lakes* trail to Smith Lake
Walk: 30—45 minutes one way
Elevation gain: 120 m (395 ft)
Maximum elevation: 1575 m (5165 ft)
Maps: Gem Trek 1:100,000 Banff & Mt. Assiniboine, and NTS 1:50,000 Castle Mountain 82-O/5 and Banff 82-O/4
Trailhead: Km 0.3 of *Twin Lakes* trail.

0.0 — Sign (elevation 1455 m). Head southeast away from old road, climbing steadily.
1.3 — Smith Lake (1575 m). A faint path circles the lake.

This short stroll leads to a small lake away from the dust and diesel, concrete and asphalt of the Trans-Canada Highway. A ramble round the lake reveals the buttresses of Castle Mountain rising to the north.

Smith Lake is named after miner and prospector Joe Smith, last resident of nearby ill-fated Silver City, where he lived until shortly before his death in 1927.

West toward Storm Mountain from Lower Twin Lake.

Arnica Lake

Distance: 7.2 km (4.4 mi) — Highway 93 South to Upper Twin Lake
Day hike/backpack: 2.5—3 hours one way
Elevation loss: 320 m (1050 ft)
Elevation gain: 585 m (1920 ft)
Maximum elevation: 2285 m (7495 ft)
Maps: Gem Trek 1:100,000 Banff & Mt. Assiniboine, and NTS 1:50,000 Mount Goodsir 82 N/1 and Banff 82-O/4
Trailhead: Parking area, with view of Vista Lake, on south side of Highway 93 South, 8.0 km (5.0 mi) west of Castle Junction and 2.0 km (1.2 mi) east of the Alberta/British Columbia boundary in Vermilion Pass.

0.0 — Trailhead kiosk (elevation 1695 m). Descend from east side of parking area on wide, well-graded path.
1.4 — East end of Vista Lake (1570 m). Cross footbridge over Altrude Creek at outlet and begin steep climb up open area.
4.0 — Enter forest.
4.2 — Unnamed pond.
4.6 — Trail becomes more gradual in basin of Arnica Lake.
5.0 — Arnica Lake (2155 m). Trail continues to southeast, climbing steadily.
5.8 — Saddle (2285 m) in northeast spur of Storm Mountain. Descend steadily.
7.2 — Upper Twin Lake (2090 m) and backcountry campground. *Twin Lakes* trail, with access to *Gibbon Pass* trail, continues south.

The presence of its namesake flowers along the trail and at the lake adds to the appeal of this hike to Arnica Lake. It is a strenuous outing, so stopping to appreciate the arnicas and other flora can be welcome.

The outing starts with a descent through forest regenerating after the large 1968 Vermilion Pass fire. The wildlife that frequents the profuse vegetation now established among the stark standing snags includes Wilson's warblers. These bright green and yellow bundles of energy (males have a small black cap) can be observed momentarily flying in place as they search for insects. Mammals such as pika, porcupine, and moose use the area; there is even beaver browse on some small trembling aspens high above Vista Lake in a rockslide zone.

Despite its name, there isn't much of a view at Vista Lake. It is, however, a good spot to rest before the climb ahead. After crossing Altrude Creek at the lake's outlet, commence the steep ascent up a mostly open slope on what can be a very hot stretch. The views can help to dispel any discomfort: highlights include the tiers of Castle Mountain to the east, and later the summit of Mt. Hector far to the north near Lake Louise.

Don't be deceived by a small, shallow body of water reached shortly after going into the trees: Arnica Lake is still a bit farther and a bit higher. Once at its shore, enjoy a well-deserved rest at this charming tarn lying close in against the sheer, dark cliffs of Storm Mountain's east face.

It is highly recommended to extend a day hike to the saddle less than a kilo-

Cirrus clouds and ridge of Storm Mountain from saddle above Arnica Lake.

metre south of the lake. For the best panorama, which includes Twin Lakes and Mt. Assiniboine, head up the ridge southwest of the saddle until break out above the grove of subalpine larches.

Although the scramble over scree and loose rock to the summit of Storm Mountain lies in Kootenay National Park, the top of that Bow Valley landmark can give a superb perspective over a vast expanse of backcountry Banff. (It's 'can give' because there is always the possibility that this peak will live up to its name, so that even in July—as happened for the author on an Alpine Club of Canada trip—a snowstorm can obscure the surroundings.)

Another connection of Storm Mountain with Banff is that famous outfitter Tom Wilson acted as guide for two surveyors on the 1889 first ascent. The magnificent northeast ridge is a classic roped mountaineering route.

Boom Lake

Distance: 5.1 km (3.2 mi) — Highway 93 South to Boom Lake
Day hike: 1.5—2 hours one way
Elevation gain: 170 m (560 ft)
Maximum elevation: 1895 m (6215 ft)
Maps: Gem Trek 1:100,000 Banff & Mt. Assiniboine, and NTS 1:50,000 Mount Goodsir 82 N/1 and Lake Louise 82 N/8
Trailhead: Parking area on north side of Highway 93 South, 7.1 km (4.4 mi) west of Castle Junction and 3.0 km (1.9 mi) east of the Alberta/British Columbia boundary in Vermilion Pass.

0.0 — Trailhead kiosk (elevation 1725 m). Cross footbridge over Boom Creek and veer north after 100 metres. Ascend gradually.
2.3 — Keep straight; *Taylor Lake* trail to right.
4.7 — Keep straight; short spur to left leads to a marshy viewpoint of the natural log booms after which the lake is named.
5.0 — Trail becomes faint along rocky margin.
5.1 — North shore of Boom Lake (1895 m) near its east end. Faint trail continues partway along north shore.

This is an easy trail, but it can be snowbound late in spring and early in autumn due to its elevation and proximity to the continental divide.

Boom Lake's name comes from trees which drift to shallows near its east end after being felled by avalanches and carried onto the ice in winter.

Views from the lake encompass Boom Mountain (best lighting for photography is in the morning) and rugged peaks along the Alberta/B.C. boundary. Among the latter are Mt. Quadra and Bident Mountain, which appear much different than in the more usual view from the north.

A path that becomes progressively fainter runs about two-thirds of the way along the north shore before finally disappearing at a small cliff that plunges into the lake. Ambitous cross-country travellers can connect with Consolation Pass by climbing steeply to above the trees and traversing high on open slopes. Be aware that there is a steep drop on the north side of the pass (see the author's *Hiking Lake Louise*).

Boom Lake.

Taylor Lake

Distance: 7.5 km (4.7 mi) — *Boom Lake* trail to *Taylor Lake from Trans-Canada Highway* trail
Day hike/backpack: 2.5—3 hours one way
Elevation gain: 340 m (1115 ft)
Elevation loss: 95 m (310 ft)
Maximum elevation: 2165 m (7100 ft)
Maps: Gem Trek 1:100,000 Banff & Mt. Assiniboine and NTS 1:50,000 Lake Louise 82 N/8
Trailhead: Km 2.3 of *Boom Lake* trail.

0.0 — Sign (elevation 1825 m). Climb steeply north on narrow path.
2.0 — Grade moderates; traverse northwest.
4.7 — High point (2165 m).
5.9 — Keep straight; O'Brien Lake 500 metres to west.
7.5 — *Taylor Lake from Trans-Canada Highway* trail (2070 m); Taylor Lake and backcountry campground 300 metres to left, Trans-Canada Highway 6.0 km to right (see *Hiking Lake Louise*).

This seldom-used trail switchbacks up steeply from the *Boom Lake* trail to round a spur of Mt. Bell. It then stays more-or-less on a contour as it turns northwest to eventually reach the junction for O'Brien Lake.

Just 1.9 km farther lies Taylor Lake and a backcountry campground. From there the options include descent to the Trans-Canada Highway, continuation north on a vague trail east of Panorama Ridge to Moraine Lake, or the off-trail trip to Taylor Pass. (See the author's *Hiking Lake Louise*, published by Luminous Compositions, for details.)

Western anemone.

Hector Lake

Distance: 2.1 km (1.3 mi) — Icefields Parkway to Hector Lake
Day hike/backpack: 30—45 minutes one way
Elevation loss: 65 m (215 ft)
Maximum elevation: 1815 m (5955 ft)
Maps: Gem Trek 1:70,000 Bow Lake and Saskatchewan Crossing, and NTS 1:50,000 Hector Lake 82 N/9
Trailhead: Small parking area on west side of Icefields Parkway, 18.0 km (11.2 mi) north of the junction with the Trans-Canada Highway and 1.0 km (0.6 mi) north of the Hector Lake interpretive viewpoint.

0.0 — Sign at north end of parking area (elevation 1815 m). Turn west and descend gradually through forest.
1.1 — Keep straight and (**caution**) ford Bow River (1750 m); *Lake Margaret* trail to left.
2.1 — East end of Hector Lake (1750 m) and backcountry campground.

This short trail leads to the largest natural lake in Banff National Park. There is even a backcountry campground: the closest to any trailhead in the park. Colourful trailblazer Jimmy Simpson once had a camp here, but any evidence of it is long gone.

The only fly in the ointment on this trip is the ford of the Bow River, which can be very difficult if not impossible in high water such as during spring melt.

As well as human anglers, western grebes frequent the lake. These water birds with an elegant black-and-white pattern need a long takeoff to get airborne, slapping their wings on the surface for a considerable distance before finally taking flight. (This requirement for a large stretch of open water sometimes causes grebes to be trapped when ice is forming.)

Hector Lake and nearby Mt. Hector are named after Sir James Hector, intrepid physician, geologist, and explorer.

Scene at ford of Bow River on *Hector Lake* trail.

Lake Margaret

Distance: 5.2 km (3.2 mi) — *Hector Lake* trail to Lake Margaret
Day hike: 1.5—2 hours one way
Elevation gain: 40 m (130 ft)
Maximum elevation: 1790 m (5870 ft)
Maps: Gem Trek 1:70,000 Bow Lake and Saskatchewan Crossing, and NTS 1:50,000 Hector Lake 82 N/9
Trailhead: Km 1.1 of *Hector Lake* trail.

0.0 — Turn south before ford of Bow River (elevation 1750 m). Follow path, vague at times, over delta.
1.0 — Ford Bow River (**caution**) below its outlet from Hector Lake. Follow along south shore of lake.
4.8 — Turn left away from lakeshore up beside stream from Lake Margaret.
5.2 — Lake Margaret (1790 m).

The outing to Lake Margaret involves what can be a daunting crossing of the Bow River, and takes a trail that is sketchy at times. Along the south shore of Hector Lake, it is best at times to travel at water's edge if possible, rather than trying to keep to the intermittent path.

Shortly after passing through several avalanche paths off Pulpit Peak, reach the outlet stream from Lake Margaret. The trail to the lake climbs through forest to arrive at its northeast corner. Lake Margaret is almost completely surrounded by rocky buttresses and ringed by coniferous trees, including some tall whitebark pines.

Beyond, in a cirque some 300 metres higher, lies Turquoise Lake: an attractive name, but getting there calls for roped travel.

A highlight as returning to the trailhead from Lake Margaret is the view—often with a reflection in Hector Lake—of Mt. Hector. Its long northwest ridge leads to the summit elevation of 3394 m (11,135 ft). There is a glimpse of the extensive glacier on Mt. Hector's north slopes, a feature not visible in the usual view of sheer cliffs seen from the south.

Crowfoot Pass and Bow Peak reflected in Hector Lake along *Lake Margaret* **trail.**

Crowfoot Pass

Distance: 6.6 km (4.1 mi) — Icefields Parkway to Mt. Balfour viewpoint
Day hike: 2—2.5 hours one way
Elevation loss: 100 m (330 ft)
Elevation gain: 535 m (1755 ft)
Maximum elevation: 2375 m (7790 ft)
Maps: Gem Trek 1:70,000 Bow Lake and Saskatchewan Crossing, and NTS 1:50,000 Hector Lake 82 N/9
Trailhead: Unmarked point on south side of Icefields Parkway 7.5 km (4.7 mi) north of Mosquito Creek bridge (350 metres west of large sign on north side of highway indicating viewpoint in 1500 m), or 1.3 km (0.8 mi) south of Crowfoot Glacier interpretive viewpoint.

0.0 — Unmarked point (elevation 1940 m). Descend gradually, heading southeast, and pick up faint path running southeast along shore of Bow Lake.
0.9 — Ford Bow River (**caution**) at outlet from Bow Lake (1925 m). On far side, trail runs south above river.
2.0 — Cross tributary and begin steep climb.
4.9 — Crowfoot Pass (2355 m). Trail continues to south.
6.1 — Low point (2270 m). Climb to ridge.
6.6 — Mt. Balfour viewpoint (2375 m).

North from Crowfoot Pass to (l to r) Cirque Peak, Dolomite Peak, and ridge of Bow Peak.

East face of Mt. Balfour from viewpoint.

This is an outing for the adventurous, since the start is ambiguous and since the trip involves a potentially hazardous ford. (Be aware that the depth of the ford can increase suddenly over the course of a hot summer day, so that it could be even more difficult on the return.) Yet the rewards are great, including a spectacular vista of a dramatic peak draped with cascading iceflows.

Arrival at two small lakes heralds the pass, from which there are views south to such landmarks as Mt. Temple, Storm Mountain, and even Mt. Assiniboine far in the distance. As impressive as this scene is, it is highly recommended to continue to the Mt. Balfour viewpoint.

It is only a matter of another 1.7 km, and although lose some elevation only to have to regain it and a bit more, it is most definitely worthwhile. This is attested to by the enthusiastic entry in the author's journal: "Stupendous panorama of eastern aspect of Balfour...extensive glaciers, thundering waterfalls, braided valley flats." The best lighting for photography from the viewpoint is in the morning, with the sun from the east.

Another possible extension from Crowfoot Pass is the scramble route up the west slopes of Bow Peak to its summit. Despite its rather diminutive height of 2868 m (9409 ft), this mountain offers a superb vantage point, particularly over Hector Lake and toward Mt. Hector. The first recorded climb of Bow Peak was by Walter Wilcox and R.L. Barrett in 1896.

Bow Glacier Falls

Distance: 4.5 km (2.8 mi) — Num-Ti-Jah Lodge to base of Bow Glacier Falls
Day hike: 1.5—2 hours one way
Elevation gain: 170 m (560 ft)
Elevation loss: 10 m (33 ft)
Maximum elevation: 2100 m (6890 ft)
Maps: Gem Trek 1:70,000 Bow Lake and Saskatchewan Crossing, and NTS 1:50,000 Hector Lake 82 N/9
Trailhead: Parking area near end of spur road to Num-Ti-Jah Lodge west off the Icefields Parkway, 3.0 km (1.9 mi) north of the Crowfoot Glacier viewpoint and 5.0 km (3.1 mi) south of the Bow Summit junction.

0.0 — Head west from parking area (elevation 1940 m) past lodge and follow along lakeshore.

2.6 — Northwest corner of Bow Lake. Continue southwest over gravel flats, crossing a small headland and aiming for north side of small canyon.

3.2 — Climb steeply up narrow path.

3.4 — High point above canyon (2010 m) opposite large chockstone forming a natural bridge. Descend to west.

3.6 — Edge of moraine basin at upstream end of canyon (2000 m). Take faint path to west toward falls; it soon fades, however, requiring individual navigation over the rough terrain.

4.5 — Base of Bow Glacier Falls (2100 m).

This hike is quite short and easily accessible, but with a wild character never-theless, leading close to a wildly leaping and tumbling waterfall. The cascades are much better appreciated when directly in their spray than when viewed from a distance.

The section along the north shore of Bow Lake is an easy ramble with open views toward the Bow Glacier and sharply pointed St. Nicholas Peak (named after the birthplace of Swiss guide Peter Sarbach).

Beyond lie Bow Glacier Falls, which originate in a fair-sized lake (not visible from below, but see next page) that lies in a basin below the receding toe of the Bow Glacier. Photographs from the early 20th century show that the ice once flowed right over the cliffs down which these waters now hasten.

Reflection in Bow Lake of view from *Bow Glacier Falls* trail: (l to r) Mt. Olive, St. Nicholas Peak, and Bow Glacier with Bow Glacier Falls below.

Bow Hut

Distance: 3.8 km (2.4 mi) — *Bow Glacier Falls* trail to Bow Hut
Off-trail scramble: 1.5—2 hours one way
Elevation gain: 440 m (1445 ft)
Maximum elevation: 2440 m (8005 ft)
Maps: Gem Trek 1:70,000 Bow Lake and Saskatchewan Crossing, and NTS 1:50,000 Hector Lake 82 N/9
Trailhead: Km 3.6 of *Bow Glacier Falls* trail.

0.0 — East edge of moraine basin at upper end of small canyon (elevation 2000 m). Cross two streams to pick up rough path east of canyon on stream flowing from south.
3.2 — Bend sharply to west and climb steeply through rockband.
3.8 — Bow Hut (2440 m) at grid reference 353204.

Although most of the Alpine Club of Canada's mountain huts are in remote locations and are intended primarily for use by climbers, Bow Hut is accessible to the scrambling fraternity. Reservations for an overnight stay are made through the ACC National Office at phone (403) 678-3200, fax (403) 678-3224, or by mail to P.O. Box 8040, Canmore, Alberta, Canada T1W 2T8. The website: www.alpineclubofcanada.ca.

There are two fords shortly after leaving the *Bow Glacier Falls* trail en route to Bow Hut, then follow a faint trail above and to the east of the canyon of the stream coming down from the south. At the head of the valley, turn west and scramble up steep slopes. (Take care to stay well clear of the danger of avalanches or icefall from the hanging glacier above. Also be aware that snow stays late into summer on much of this route.)

The present Bow Hut was built in 1989 to replace an older structure—now gone—that stood higher up and closer to the glacier and the Wapta Icefield.

An option is to visit the source of Bow Glacier Falls: the lake at the base of the receding toe of the Bow Glacier. This body of turquoise water can be reached by taking the obvious ramp on the west side of the canyon below Bow Hut. Descent back to established trails is by way of a route marked with rock cairns that passes through small cliff bands and along a well-defined lateral moraine.

Bow Hut.

Bow Summit Fire Lookout Site

Distance: 2.9 km (1.8 mi) — Bow Summit parking area to site of former fire look-out
Day hike: 1—1.5 hour(s) one way
Elevation gain: 260 m (855 ft)
Elevation loss: 15 m (50 ft)
Maximum elevation: 2315 m (7595 ft)
Maps: Gem Trek 1:70,000 Bow Lake and Saskatchewan Crossing, and NTS 1:50,000 Blaeberry River 82 N/10 and Hector Lake 82 N/9
Trailhead: Parking area to right 400 metres after turning west off Icefields Parkway at Bow Summit junction, 5.0 km (3.1 mi) north of Num-Ti-Jah Lodge junction and 16.5 km (10.2 mi) south of Waterfowl Lakes frontcountry campground. (The upper parking area is reserved for buses and disabled persons.)

0.0 — Sign (elevation 2070 m). Follow paved path.
0.1 — Keep straight; to right loops back to parking area.
0.6 — Turn left; Peyto Lake viewpoint to right, upper parking area hard left.
0.7 — Keep straight (2135 m); *Peyto Lake* trail to right.
0.8 — Keep left; to right is interpretive loop (a recommended option), hard left is connector to upper parking area.
1.0 — Head south up old roadway; paved interpretive loop to right.
2.3 — Road begins short gradual descent (2270 m).
2.5 — Low point (2255 m).
2.9 — Site of former fire lookout (2315 m).

Most park visitors are familiar with the famous viewpoint over Peyto Lake at Bow Summit, and many know of the adjacent interpretive loop. But few realize that there is a short, easily graded trail nearby that gives an unexpected view to the south (though the author's *Fire Lookout Hikes in the Canadian Rockies*, published by Luminous Compositions in 1998, increased awareness of this and many other similarly rewarding hikes).

So if inclined to stretch the legs a bit and want to experience a little-known hike, take this former access road to the site of a fire lookout (the building has been removed). Along the way are views of peaks to the east and southeast, including Cirque Peak, the towers of Dolomite Peak, and heavily glaciated Mt. Hector. A surprise awaits at the end of the trail, for here the upper expanse of the Crowfoot Glacier and below it the full length of Bow Lake suddenly come into view.

As returning over this little gem of a trail, the profusion of wildflowers in the upper subalpine meadows can be enjoyed. The species to be found include arnica, paintbrush, alpine speedwell, heathers, fireweed, and cinquefoil.

Peyto Lake

Distance: 2.3 km (1.4 mi) — *Bow Summit Fire Lookout Site* trail to Peyto Lake
Day hike: 30—45 minutes one way
Elevation loss: 290 m (950 ft)
Maximum elevation: 2135 m (7005 ft)
Maps: Gem Trek 1:70,000 Bow Lake and Saskatchewan Crossing, and NTS
1:50,000 Blaeberry River 82 N/10
Trailhead: Km 0.7 of *Bow Summit Fire Lookout Site* trail.

0.0 — Sign (elevation 2135 m). Descend to southwest off paved path.
2.3 — Southeast corner of Peyto Lake (1845 m).

     This trail drops steeply from near the Peyto (properly pronounced "pea-toe") Lake viewpoint to reach the southeast corner of the lake. It's easy to go down, but keep in mind that it's a stiff haul back up.

     The lake gets its name from Ebenezer William (Bill) Peyto, famous guide, outfitter, and early park warden. The story goes that Bill, a rugged individualist, didn't like it if even one other person showed up at the wilderness camp at Bow Lake. With the statement "There's too darn many people around here, I'm going where there's some peace and quiet," he would leave to bivouac alone at Bow Pass, above the body of water that came to bear his name.

     The final section of this trail switchbacks down a narrow avalanche chute. Once at the bottom, it is intriguing to explore the delta formed by outwash material. On the lake might be seen waterfowl such as buffleheads: small diving ducks in which the males look particularly striking in their distinctive black-and-white plumage.

     Another trail leads from a small parking area on the west side of the Icefields Parkway, 2.6 km (1.6 mi) north of the Bow Summit junction, down to the east shore of Peyto Lake in 1.4 km, but it dead-ends there. (Backcountry skiers continue across the ice in winter.)

     An option from the end of this trail is to go on to Caldron Lake: see p. 120.

View from *Peyto Lake* trail of south end of lake and of delta.

Caldron Lake

Distance: 5.1 km (3.2 mi) — Peyto Lake to Caldron Lake
Off-trail scramble: 2—2.5 hours one way
Elevation gain: 555 m (1820 ft)
Elevation loss: 40 m (130 ft)
Maximum elevation: 2400 m (7870 ft)
Maps: Gem Trek 1:70,000 Bow Lake and Saskatchewan Crossing, and NTS 1:50,000 Blaeberry River 82 N/10
Trailhead: End of *Peyto Lake* trail at km 2.3 (see p. 119).

0.0 — Southeast corner of Peyto Lake (elevation 1845 m). Head southwest over flats.

1.0 — Start of small canyon. Keep south at edge of flats.

2.3 — Start of rocky canyon. Follow faint path on east side of stream.

2.6 — Cross to west side of stream on primitive footbridge. Angle up to northwest to base of lateral moraine (some cairns mark route).

3.0 — Pick up faint path just to west of crest of lateral moraine near its base.

3.5 — Top of lateral moraine. Veer to southwest; Peyto Glacier to south.

4.6 — High point (2400 m) on faint path above cliffs (may be snow-covered). Descend to northwest and make way over bouldery terrain.

5.1 — East end of Caldron Lake (2360 m).

Caldron Lake and summit of Mistaya Mountain.

Southeast from Caldron Lake with Mt. Jimmy Simpson in distance on left and Mt. Thompson with Dragonback Glacier on right.

This off-trail outing leads to a body of water with a mysterious-sounding name.

To reach Caldron Lake, head southwest from the end of the *Peyto Lake* trail, travelling over gravel flats toward a small gorge at the edge of a wooded knoll jutting out from the east. It is usually feasible to stay beside the water; otherwise, an old path begins some 200 metres east of the start of the gorge and goes over the ridge through forest.

Smaller flats lie beyond the narrows, then a tighter gorge that has a faint path along the east side. This leads to a rudimentary bridge over the stream (continuing up the east side not recommended).

A cairned route leads steeply up a sharp-crested lateral moraine. Veering west at the top and continuing to climb leads to the main difficulty of this route: a traverse above a cliff band (do not go on without an ice axe if there is snow on this section). A slight descent and the crossing of an area of large boulders sees arrival at the east end of Caldron Lake.

The open terrain in this hanging valley invites further exploration, such as to the north for better views of Mt. Patterson. Such a jaunt will also give views back over the entire lake (including the peninsula on its south shore, formed by a moraine) and to the glaciated north face of Peyto Peak.

The supernatural atmosphere suggested by the name of Caldron Lake is augmented by the name of the tongue of ice to the southeast on the north face of Mt. Thompson: the Dragonback Glacier.

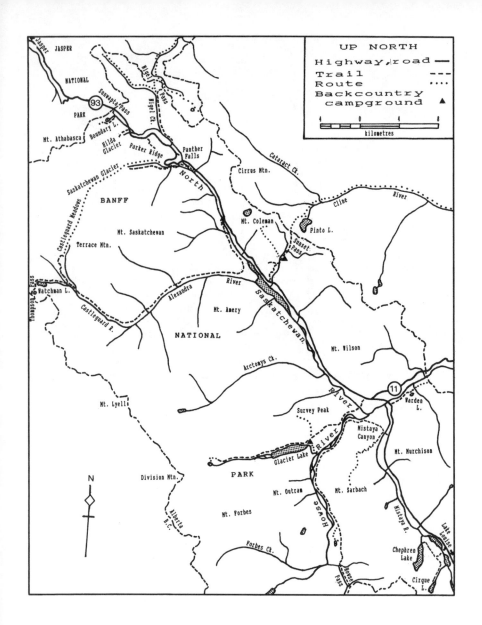

122

Up North

Cirrus Mountain from side path at km 0.6 of *Old "Wonder Trail."*

123

Chephren Lake

Distance: 3.5 km (2.2 mi) — Waterfowl Lakes frontcountry campground to Chephren Lake
Day hike: 1—1.5 hour(s) one way
Elevation gain: 90 m (295 ft)
Elevation loss: 40 m (130 ft)
Maximum elevation: 1760 m (5775 ft)
Maps: Gem Trek 1:70,000 Bow Lake and Saskatchewan Crossing, and NTS 1:50,000 Mistaya Lake 82 N/15
Trailhead: Waterfowl Lakes frontcountry campground, west off the Icefields Parkway 16.5 km (10.2 mi) north of the Bow Summit junction and 18.0 km (11.2 mi) south of the highway bridge over the North Saskatchewan River. Enter the campground at the attendant's kiosk and keep straight to the Mistaya River, then turn right to parking area.

0.0 — Trailhead kiosk (elevation 1670 m). Cross footbridge over Mistaya River and climb southwest.
1.3 — Turn right (1740 m) on less well-defined trail; *Cirque Lake* trail to left.
2.1 — High point (1760 m). Boggy sections.
3.2 — Trail turns sharply southwest.
3.5 — Northeast end of Chephren Lake (1720 m).

As crossing the solid log footbridge over the Mistaya River at the start of this hike, look northeast to get an impressive view of rock towers and pinnacles above Noyes Creek.

The well-established trail leads to a T-junction in a little over 1 km: keep right and climb gradually. Crest a low saddle and drop a little to travel through a swampy area before making a sharp turn left 300 metres before the lake.

Chephren Lake, which is over 2 km long, lies hard against the southeastern cliffs of Mt. Chephren. The names of these features derive from the son and successor of Cheops, who was responsible for the construction of the Great Pyramid in Egypt. The mountain was originally called Black Pyramid but was renamed to avoid confusion with Pyramid Mountain near Jasper townsite. The adjacent White Pyramid was named by illustrious alpinist J. Norman Collie after its symmetrical crown of snow and ice.

The precipitous east face of Howse Peak cleaves the air above the far end of Chephren Lake. The name of this peak is affiliated with Howse Pass, which is a mere 5 km to the west as the raven flies but considerably farther on foot (see *Howse Pass* trail description, p. 128).

Cirque Lake

Distance: 2.9 km (1.8 mi) — *Chephren Lake* trail to Cirque Lake
Day hike: 45 minutes—1 hour one way
Elevation gain: 55 m (180 ft)
Maximum elevation: 1795 m (5890 ft)
Maps: Gem Trek 1:70,000 Bow Lake and Saskatchewan Crossing, and NTS 1:50,000 Mistaya Lake 82 N/15
Trailhead: Km 1.3 of *Chephren Lake* trail.

0.0 — Sign (elevation 1740 m). Turn left; *Chephren Lake* trail to right. Ascend gradually.
2.9 — North end of Cirque Lake (1795 m).

This hike is more strenuous than that to Chephren Lake, taking a rocky, rooty trail that is slippery when wet. The route passes through coniferous forest for most of its length, yet can offer much in the way of subtle sights. Travel beside a small stream reveals a series of low waterfalls, and on the forest floor are the evergreen runners of plants commonly known as ground pine: members of the ancient and primitive genus *Lycopodium*.

Bird species that might be observed include such year-round residents as boreal chickadee (with brown cap, black bib, and a reddish wash on the sides) and spruce grouse. The latter has the folk name "fool hen" due to its remarkable nonchalance.

Break out into a major avalanche chute just before Cirque Lake. There are several glaciers at the lake's head, as implied by its name (moving ice having scooped out the rocky bowls called cirques). Moraine ridges descend to the south end of the lake, and glaciers hang above on the nearly vertical peaks of the continental divide.

A glimpse of a moose might be had on this outing...despite their large size, these creatures are able to disappear quickly into surrounding vegetation.

A visit combining this trail with the *Chephren Lake* trail creates an outing with a total distance of 12.8 km (7.9 mi).

Bull moose.

Mistaya Canyon

Distance: 0.5 km (0.3 mi) — Icefields Parkway to Mistaya Canyon
Walk: 10—15 minutes one way
Elevation loss: 40 m (130 ft)
Maximum elevation: 1520 m (4985 ft)
Maps: Gem Trek 1:70,000 Bow Lake and Saskatchewan Crossing, and NTS 1:50,000 Mistaya Lake 82 N/15
Trailhead: Parking area on west side of Icefields Parkway, 14.5 km (9.0 mi) north of the entrance to Waterfowl Lakes frontcountry campground and 4.0 km (2.5 mi) south of the bridge over the North Saskatchewan River.

0.0 — Trailhead kiosk (elevation 1520 m). Descend on trail from north end of parking area.
0.5 — Bridge over Mistaya Canyon (1480 m).

This short stroll down to a footbridge over a canyon of the Mistaya River gives graphic illustrations of the erosive power of flowing water. The curves and meanders of the river (whose name is a Native word for grizzly bear) are replicated in rock. The downrushing river has carved a deep, narrow slot through limestone; pebbles and rocks swirled by water have created numerous potholes. There is also a small natural bridge.

Keep safety in mind if leave the trail to explore here.

Start of Mistaya Canyon; false peak of Mt. Sarbach in distance.

Sarbach Fire Lookout Site

Distance: 4.9 km (3.0 mi) — Mistaya Canyon to site of former fire lookout on Mt. Sarbach
Day hike: 2—2.5 hours one way
Elevation gain: 565 m (1855 ft)
Maximum elevation: 2045 m (6710 ft)
Maps: Gem Trek 1:70,000 Bow Lake and Saskatchewan Crossing, and NTS 1:50,000 Mistaya Lake 82 N/15
Trailhead: End of *Mistaya Canyon* trail.

0.0 — Sign (elevation 1480 m) at west end of bridge over Mistaya Canyon. Turn right and climb steadily.
0.2 — Turn left (1490 m); *Howse Pass* trail straight ahead. Climb steadily at first, then more steeply.
4.9 — Site (2045 m) of former fire lookout on northeast ridge of Mt. Sarbach.

This unrelentingly steep hike leads to an open area above treeline that was once the site of a fire lookout. The route gives some views of the Mistaya River at first; however, it is in forest for most of its length.

That is not to say that there is nothing to see: in spring, for example, can be found clusters of calypso orchids, their colours and shape aptly matching their tropical-sounding name. Later in the season, white camas (a member of the lily family) and heart-leaved arnica border the path.

Given the elevation of over 2000 m, snow stays late near the small clearing at trail's end. Neatly placed rocks marking a network of paths here indicate the care taken by lookout staff in earlier times.

Below the lookout site flow three rivers: the Mistaya, with wild whitewater and steep east bank; the wide, much-braided Howse; and—augmented by these two tributaries—the North Saskatchewan, rolling down from the north, then suddenly veering east.

Across the valley rises many-tiered Mt. Murchison, whose elevation is 3337 m (10,945 ft): it was once thought to be the highest peak in the Canadian Rockies. The ethereal cascades of Murchison Falls, which plunge almost 250 metres over a sudden scarp above treeline, grace its east flank.

Although most parties require a rope to reach the summit of Mt. Sarbach, it is possible to venture off-trail onto the northeast ridge without getting into technical terrain. For details, see the author's *Ridgewalks in the Canadian Rockies* (Luminous Compositions, 2001).

Howse Pass

Distance: 25.3 km (15.7 mi) — *Sarbach Fire Lookout Site* trail to Howse Pass
Backpack: 1.5—2 days one way
Elevation loss: 120 m (395 ft)
Elevation gain: 165 m (540 ft)
Maximum elevation: 1580 m (5180 ft)
Maps: Gem Trek 1:70,000 Bow Lake and Saskatchewan Crossing, and NTS 1:50,000 Mistaya Lake 82 N/15
Trailhead: Km 0.2 of *Sarbach Fire Lookout Site* trail (see p. 127).

0.0 — Sign (elevation 1490 m). Keep straight; *Sarbach Fire Lookout Site* trail to left. Descend gradually through forest.

3.5 — Keep straight; horse trail from Saskatchewan River Crossing (involves ford of Mistaya River) comes in on right.

3.7 — Howse River flats (1425 m). Mostly level going.

5.2 — Turn south at major bend in river.

7.2 — Random camping site and stream crossing.

13.5 — Travel over open flats; shifting river channels may have washed out sections of trail.

15.0 — Re-enter forest and climb gradually.

18.5 — Keep straight after stream crossing; trail to left leads to site of former warden cabin and roundabout connector to Lagoon Lake.

21.7 — High point (1580 m).

22.5 — Turn left and cross stream (1525 m); warden cabin to right.

25.1 — Cross stream flowing from west side of Howse Peak.

25.3 — Howse Pass (1535 m) and Alberta/British Columbia boundary. Rough trail continues south and links with logging road in Blaeberry Valley.

This trail opens up early in the hiking season because of its low elevation. Even though the pass itself is forested and does not offer expansive views, it holds significant historical interest.

Glacier lilies photographed at Howse Pass.

View from Survey Peak over valley of Howse River toward Howse Pass.

The first documented non-Natives to traverse Howse Pass were in a North West Company party led by renowned geographer David Thompson. They crossed in 1807 en route to establishing the first fur trade post in the Columbia Valley to the west.

Interestingly, Joseph Howse, the Hudson's Bay Company employee after whom the pass is named, did not cross it until two years later. These early nineteenth-century travellers reported sightings and sign of bison in the vicinity of the pass, but the animals were soon killed (as indeed were all bison in the Canadian Rockies).

Of course, the route over Howse Pass was long known to the Native people of the area, as acknowledged in the citation on the Historical Sites and Monuments Board of Canada plaque at the pass. It was a blockade of Howse Pass by Piegans that resulted in the use of Athabasca Pass, some 120 km to the north, as a main trade link. As a result, this pass returned to obscurity and has remained essentially undisturbed, although a logging road reaches within 10 km on the unprotected British Columbia side.

The Howse Valley, with its open flats and braided channels flanked by steep wooded slopes and glaciated peaks, is sanctuary to diverse wildlife. Mammals that might be seen, or of which sign could be found, include marten, black bear, and wolf. (The author had a memorable sighting of five wolves on the flats during an overnight winter trip.)

The bird species that can be observed in the area include Canada goose, belted kingfisher, greater yellowlegs, bufflehead, blue-winged teal, and the ubiquitous mallard. Red-tailed hawks may nest in the valley, so their territorial piercing calls might be heard.

The trail toward Freshfield Lake involves several potentially risky fords. Any use this trail does get is usually by mountaineers, and that traffic has diminished since the removal of the climbing hut near Niverville Meadows. The route shown on some maps as going up Forbes Creek has long been unmaintained and so is blocked by much windfall.

Warden Lake

Distance: 2.2 km (1.4 mi) — Icefields Parkway to Warden Lake
Walk: 30—45 minutes one way
Elevation gain: Negligible
Maximum elevation: 1390 m (4560 ft)
Maps: Gem Trek 1:70,000 Bow Lake and Saskatchewan Crossing, and NTS 1:50,000 Mistaya Lake 82 N/15
Trailhead: Short gravel access road on southwest side of Icefields Parkway opposite Saskatchewan River Crossing warden station, 3.1 km (1.9 mi) north of Mistaya Canyon parking area and 0.5 km (0.3 mi) south of bridge over North Saskatchewan River. Trail starts on opposite, northeast side of pavement.

0.0 — Sign (elevation 1390 m). Head east on path.
0.2 — Turn right onto old road; warden station to left.
1.9 — Turn right; old road ahead has been rehabilitated.
2.2 — Northwest corner of Warden Lake (1390 m).

    This short, level walk along the North Saskatchewan River is of particular interest botanically, especially in early summer when many wildflowers bloom on the open flats. Because of the low elevation, many species appear here before anywhere else in Banff National Park. Among the possibilities are bird's-eye primrose, shooting star, elephanthead, yellow mountain avens, and butterwort.

    An intriguing sighting at Warden Lake, most likely during spring migration, could be one of two species of phalarope: Wilson's or red-necked. These shorebirds feed by spinning in the water to stir up larvae, crustaceans, and insects. Females do the courting, and are larger and more brightly plumaged than the males, which take responsibility for incubating the eggs and raising the young.

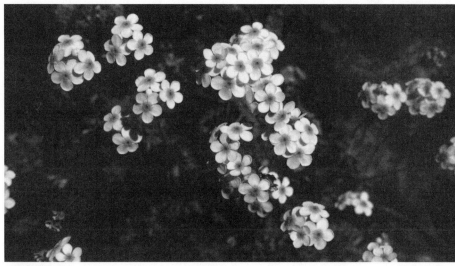

Rock jasmine.

Glacier Lake

Distance: 19.9 km (12.2 mi) — Icefields Parkway to moraine above Southeast Lyell Glacier
Day hike/backpack: 7—8 hours one way
Elevation gain: 685 m (2245 ft)
Elevation loss: 305 m (1000 ft)
Maximum elevation: 1830 m (6000 ft)
Maps: Gem Trek 1:70,000 Bow Lake and Saskatchewan Crossing, and NTS 1:50,000 Mistaya Lake 82 N/15
Trailhead: Parking area on south side of Icefields Parkway, 1.0 km (0.6 mi) west of Saskatchewan River Crossing at the junction with Highway 11.

0.0 — Trailhead kiosk (elevation 1450 m). Head into forest.
0.2 — Keep straight; old trail toward highway to left.
0.5 — High point (1465 m).
1.1 — Cross footbridge (1415 m) over North Saskatchewan River.
1.8 — High point (1450 m).
2.3 — Viewpoint over Howse River and Mt. Sarbach to south. Descend to west.
2.6 — West bank of Howse River (1420 m).
3.5 — Begin ascent of tributary stream: five footbridges in next 1.6 km.
5.9 — High point (1660 m). Descend steadily.
8.2 — Keep straight; old trail toward Howse River to left.
8.6 — Keep straight; old trail toward Howse River to left.
8.9 — Keep straight along north shore of Glacier Lake (1435 m); backcountry campground 150 metres to left.
12.6 — West end of Glacier Lake. Faint trail continues upvalley; fords may be required in places where it has washed out.
17.2 — Old campsite with collapsed log tripod.
18.3 — Begin steep climb up to crest of lateral moraine on overgrown path.
19.9 — End of defined path (1830 m) above grassy ramp leading down toward toe of Southeast Lyell Glacier. Vague route heads uphill to north.

Although the first historical record of this lake comes from David Thompson, who visited it in June, 1807, Glacier Lake owes its name to James Hector, who camped by it in 1858 during explorations as a member of the Palliser Expedition.

Tha name is certainly appropriate, for there are several glaciers in view from the lake and they give it the characteristic turquoise hue. Minute particles known as "rock flour" that are ground up by the slowly moving rivers of ice are carried into glacially-fed lakes, where they remain in suspension and reflect a blue-green colour.

The backcountry campground at the east end of Glacier Lake serves as an excellent base for further wanderings. Its cable storage system provides a safe place to store food and other scented objects from the black bears that frequent the area. There is a small, decrepit cabin near the start of the path up to the cables.

A well-defined trail continues to the western end of the lake, mostly staying close to the north shore. It does slant up slightly at one stage to pass (cont. p. 132)

Reflection of Division Mountain in Glacier Lake.

(cont. from p. 131) through an avalanche path, now vegetated with trembling aspen and some substantial birch trees.

Proceeding west up the wide meadows beyond the end of the lake, sections of trail may have been wiped out by new channels, thus requiring a ford or fords. The most obvious trail after an old campsite climbs through an overgrown section to the crest of a high, steep lateral moraine. This affords a dramatic perspective over an incredibly rugged landscape of icefalls, seracs, crevasses, moraines, and cliffs. It is possible to scramble down a relatively gradual ramp to examine the toe of the Southeast Lyell Glacier.

A trip for experienced off-trail travellers is the ascent of Survey Peak via the drainage north of the east end of Glacier Lake. A faint path starts up from approximately 100 metres east of the junction for the backcountry campground. It continues for about 1 km, rising some 150 metres to an open ridge that gives a view of the entire length of Glacier Lake.

Beyond this point, forge a route through thick vegetation and up steep scree slopes to reach the cairn on the summit of Survey Peak. This point—elevation 2665 m (8740 ft)—was first reached in 1898 by J.N. Collie and H.E.M. Stutfield, who used it to map the surroundings. The panoramic view suggested by the name includes the sharp final ridges of Mt. Forbes, named by Hector after his professor of natural history at the University of Edinburgh.

Sunset Fire Lookout Site

Distance: 4.5 km (2.8 mi) — Icefields Parkway to site of former fire lookout on edge of cliffs south of Mt. Coleman
Day hike: 1.5—2 hours one way
Elevation gain: 585 m (1920 ft)
Elevation loss: 40 m (130 ft)
Maximum elevation: 2025 m (6640 ft)
Maps: Gem Trek 1:70,000 Bow Lake and Saskatchewan Crossing, and NTS 1:50,000 Cline River 83 C/2
Trailhead: Parking area on north side of Icefields Parkway, 4.4 km (2.7 mi) north of entrance to Rampart Creek youth hostel and 18.2 km (11.3 mi) south of the parking area on the Big Bend.

0.0 — Trailhead kiosk (elevation 1440 m). Climb, moderately at first, then more steeply.
2.9 — Turn left (1830 m); *Sunset Pass* trail straight ahead. Continue climbing.
4.3 — High point (2025 m).
4.5 — Site of former fire lookout (1985 m).

This very steep trail climbs beside Norman Creek, with a view of a high waterfall en route. The end of the trail gives a dizzying view down to the North Saskatchewan River. As the site of a former fire lookout (for more info, see the author's *Fire Lookout Hikes in the Canadian Rockies*), it naturally offers other views too. These include west up the valley of the Alexandra River (see *Castleguard Meadows* trail, p. 136), and south to the glaciated massif of Mt. Wilson. The name of that 3261 m (10,696 ft) landmark north of Saskatchewan Crossing honours Tom Wilson, the affable packer and guide who was a central figure in many exploratory and mountaineering expeditions in the wilderness of Banff National Park.

There's a chance that mountain goats may be nearby at this exposed aerie, for this is a setting in keeping with the preferred haunts of those agile alpinists.

Mountain goat from end of *Sunset Fire Lookout Site* trail, with view south down valley of North Saskatchewan River including Mt. Sarbach on the right.

Sunset Pass

Distance: 5.3 km (3.3 mi) — *Sunset Fire Lookout Site* trail to Banff National Park boundary
Day hike/backpack: 1.5—2 hours one way
Elevation gain: 305 m (1000 ft)
Maximum elevation: 2135 m (7005 ft)
Maps: Gem Trek 1:70,000 Bow Lake and Saskatchewan Crossing, and NTS 1:50,000 Cline River 83 C/2
Trailhead: Km 2.9 of *Sunset Fire Lookout Site* trail (see p. 133).

0.0 — Junction (elevation 1830 m). Keep straight; *Sunset Fire Lookout Site* trail to left. Climb steadily.

1.0 — Keep right (1955 m); path to left leads to Norman Lake. (Also see *Mt. Coleman* description next page.)

1.2 — Cross log footbridge to open meadows.

1.3 — Backcountry campground. Continue north through meadows, ascending gradually.

5.3 — Banff National Park boundary (2135 m). Trail continues down through cliffband toward Pinto Lake and along Cline River to Highway 11; Pinto Lake visible from just beyond park boundary.

This trail climbs a short distance from the junction with the *Sunset Fire Lookout Site* trail before reaching the wide-open meadows that are a highlight of the Sunset Pass area. Numerous diggings give unmistakable sign of grizzly bears in this upper subalpine terrain.

Travel between Mt. Coleman and unnamed peaks to the south to reach the park boundary and an inspiring view of large Pinto Lake below. In autumn the leaves of the clumps of bearberry at Sunset Pass turn an eyecatching deep red.

A trail, muddy at times, can be taken down to Pinto Lake and out to the David Thompson Highway via the valley of the Cline River. Another option, for experienced cross-country trekkers, is to head up Cataract Creek in the provincial White Goat Wilderness Area (no horses, hunting, or fishing). There is lots of deadfall en route to Cataract Pass, from which can link with the *Nigel Pass* trail (see p. 143).

Mt. Coleman from meadows in Sunset Pass area.

Mt. Coleman

Distance: 4.8 km (3.0 mi) — *Sunset Pass* trail to summit of Mt. Coleman
Off-trail scramble: 2.5—3 hours one way
Elevation gain: 1180 m (3870 ft)
Maximum elevation: 3135 m (10,286 ft)
Maps: Gem Trek 1:70,000 Bow Lake and Saskatchewan Crossing, and NTS 1:50,000 Cline River 83 C/2
Trailhead: Km 1.0 of *Sunset Pass* trail.

0.0 — Junction (elevation 1955 m). Keep left; trail to right leads toward back-country campground and Sunset Pass.
0.5 — Path ends at south end of Norman Lake. Head around lake and northwest up through forest; once above the trees, angle up into cirque between Mt. Coleman and south spur.
3.9 — Saddle (2740 m) southwest of summit at grid reference 048735.
4.8 — Summit of Mt. Coleman (3135 m).

Keen off-trail scramblers can head up Mt. Coleman from the *Sunset Pass* trail. This peak is named for A.P. Coleman, pioneer geologist and mountaineer, who wrote evocatively of "the feeling of having made a new discovery [...] as one turns off from a scarcely-beaten trail into a route perhaps never before trodden." The clincher is, as Coleman said, that "this experience may be had in a thousand valleys among the Rockies of Canada."

Routefinding skills and a head for heights are necessary to surmount the final block and to venture along the summit ridge. (Snow will be encountered; an ice axe is necessary.) The top of Mt. Coleman reveals one of the great panoramas of Banff National Park: nearby rises the forbidding east face of Cirrus Mountain, dark rock above the sprawling white Huntingdon Glacier.

To the west on either side of the Alexandra River stand the massive blocks of Mt. Saskatchewan and Mt. Amery, both over 3300 m high. Northwest lies the region of the vast Columbia Icefield, punctuated by peaks such as Mt. Athabasca and The Twins. The vista culminates in Mt. Columbia, whose shimmering summit—elevation 3747 m (12,290 ft)—is the highest point in Alberta.

Scrambler on summit of Mt. Coleman, with east face of Cirrus Mountain and Huntington Glacier on right.

Castleguard Meadows

Distance: 35.0 km (21.7 mi) — Icefields Parkway to Castleguard Meadows
Backpack: 2—2.5 days
Elevation loss: 125 m (410 ft)
Elevation gain: 630 m (2065 ft)
Maximum elevation: 2055 m (6740 ft)
Maps: Gem Trek 1:70,000 Bow Lake and Saskatchewan Crossing [start of trail], and NTS 1:50,000 Cline River 83 C/2 and Columbia Icefield 83 C/3
Trailhead: Paved pulloff on west side of Icefields Parkway, 9.5 km (5.9 mi) north of the *Sunset Pass* trailhead and 8.7 km (4.9 mi) south of the *Saskatchewan Glacier Toe* trailhead.

0.0 — Pulloff on west side of Icefields Parkway (elevation 1525 m). Descend steep track that starts 10 metres to north.

0.1 — Cross footbridge (1515 m) over gorge of North Saskatchewan River. Head south over undulating course of former fire road.

5.4 — High point (1540 m); trail bends to west up valley of Alexandra River. Descend gradually.

10.9 — Flats (1450 m) on north side of Alexandra River.

11.7 — End of well-defined trail at new channel. If water is low, ford to flats and follow former road (vague at times), keeping north of main channel. If too deep to cross, this ford (and others farther on) can be bypassed by taking to the hillside north of the river for 500 metres.

13.5 — Cross Terrace Creek (tricky in high water). Old campsite on west side.

18.9 — Cross Castelets Creek (tricky in high water); enter gravel flats soon after.

20.5 — End of old road at sign; narrow trail enters forest and begins to climb.

20.9 — Warden cabin; trail continues to west behind cabin, now following valley of Castleguard River.

30.6 — Cross stream, possibly on notched log high above (log may be slippery).

31.6 — Cross outlet stream (1680 m) from Outram's Shower Bath waterfall; do not follow faint path (may be marked with survey tape) that leads uphill into forest. *Thompson Pass* trail starts across Castleguard River.

31.9 — Campsite 100 metres west of Outram's Shower Bath. Begin steep climb.

34.7 — High point (2055 m). Trail descends gradually to southeast.

35.0 — End of defined trail (2030 m) near small cascades. The designated camping area (with an outhouse) in this Special Preservation zone is on the hummock across the creek: camp must be made within 100 metres of the sign at approximate grid reference 857703.

The destination of this extended trip is sublime but the approach is usually uneventful, although there can be challenging fords where shifting channels of the Alexandra River may have caused washouts. Doing this trip late in the season will keep such crossings to a minimum.

The first twenty kilometres are dull walking on a former fire road; the first six kilometres especially so since they merely parallel the North Saskatchewan River opposite the highway. (This section is open to mountain biking.) If lucky, a lynx might be sighted in these remote valleys, as one was by explorer Mary Schäffer in 1907.

Otherwise, the most exciting moments on the trudge up the old road are likely to come as crossing Terrace and Castelets creeks. The trail does not continue up the Alexandra Valley toward the Alexandra Glaciers and Mt. Alexandra (these features are on NTS 1:50,000 sheet Rostrum Peak 82 N/14), rather turning northwest from the end of the abandoned road to follow the Castleguard River.

A tributary of the Alexandra, the Castleguard is nevertheless a sizable river rushing headlong down from its glacial origins. This part of the journey is in a random camping area, and there is a suitable campsite near the impressive waterfall known as Outram's Shower Bath. Sir James Outram, a member of the first party to ascend Mt. Assiniboine, wrote of this place: "we pitched our tents just within the border of the trees, in a sheltered, sunny spot, close to a splendid waterfall, which, like a smaller one a few yards distant, sprang from a subterranean channel."

Outram—who has a peak named for him near Glacier Lake—doesn't mention trying out the natural plumbing here, although the name suggests he did. He does refer, several pages earlier in his book *In the Heart of the Canadian Rockies* (1905), to "shower-baths conferred upon us by the rain-soaked bush." (The author can attest to this phenomenon, having been drenched by wet Menziesia and dwarf birch shrubs overhanging the trail on the way up the valley.)

Outram and Swiss guide Christian Kaufmann made the first ascent of Mt. Columbia in an amazing push from this camp; although less ambitious, the climb to Castleguard Meadows is taxing nonetheless. Once there, it's rewarding to revel in the remote character of the place and to savour the vistas stretching from the triple peaks of Mt. Lyell to the south around to the seldom-seen south face of Mt. Athabasca. Camp in this Special Preservation zone must be as described above.

Although there are no other outings in this book that require more than an ice axe, there is the option, if knowledgeable in glacier travel and properly equipped, of leaving the Castleguard Meadows via a descent of the Saskatchewan Glacier.

Scene in Castleguard Meadows, with south face of Mt. Athabasca in distance.

Thompson Pass

Distance: 4.5 km (2.8 mi) — *Castleguard Meadows* trail to Thompson Pass
Extension of backpack: 1.5—2 hours one way
Elevation gain: 320 m (1050 ft)
Maximum elevation: 2000 m (6560 ft)
Map: NTS 1:50,000 Columbia Icefield 83 C/3
Trailhead: Km 31.6 of *Castleguard Meadows* trail (see p. 136).

0.0 — Crossings (elevation 1680 m) of outlet of Outram's Shower Bath waterfall and of Castleguard River.

0.1 — Sign on west bank of river at entrance of trail into forest. Start steady climb.

2.1 — Northeast corner of Watchman Lake. Continue along north shore.

2.9 — Northwest corner of Watchman Lake; continue around to west end for 200 metres before beginning steep climb.

3.9 — East end of Cinema Lake; trail keeps to north.

4.5 — Thompson Pass (2000 m) and Banff National Park and Alberta/British Columbia boundary.

This is a worthwhile side trip from the *Castleguard Meadows* trail, provided that the Castleguard River at the start can be safely forded. (Keep in mind that it's fed by the Columbia Icefield not far upstream and that in warm temperatures the daily influx of meltwater may make the river too deep to cross back in the afternoon.)

The highest peak in view from Thompson Pass is to the west: Mt. Bryce—elevation 3507 m (11,503 ft). To the south is Mt. Spring-Rice, whose curious name has nothing to do with a food staple: rather, it honours British diplomat Sir Cecil Spring-Rice. Across the Castleguard Valley to the northeast stand the prominent pyramid-like peaks of Terrace Mountain and its unnamed neighbours.

Thompson Pass is named after American alpinist C.S. Thompson, who made the first recorded visit to it. The trail fades just beyond the pass. A logging road penetrates to within a couple of kilometres of the boundary from the west; contact the B.C. Forestry Service office in Golden for current info on gates and road conditions.

**Flowerrs of
Menziesia.**

Saskatchewan Glacier Toe

Distance: 7.2 km (4.4 mi) — Icefields Parkway to toe of Saskatchewn Glacier
Day hike: 2—2.5 hours one way
Elevation gain: 180 m (590 ft)
Elevation loss: 35 m (115 ft)
Maximum elevation: 1790 m (5870 ft)
Maps: Gem Trek 1:75,000 Columbia Icefield and NTS 1:50,000 Columbia Icefield 83 C/3
Trailhead: Small parking area on the south side of the Icefields Parkway, 17.5 km (10.9 mi) north of the *Sunset Fire Lookout Site* trailhead and 0.7 km (0.4 mi) east of the parking area at the westernmost point of the Big Bend.

0.0 — Old bridge (elevation 1645 m) over gorge on North Saskatchewn River. Cross and keep right on other side, following along edge of river bank; straight ahead is the hike down a section of the old "Wonder Trail" (see p. 141).

0.4 — Keep straight on old jeep track; section coming in on left starts off the old "Wonder Trail."

0.7 — Veer right off jeep track to cross flats on bulldozed swath.

1.1 — Rejoin old jeep track at base of climb over forested ridge.

1.9 — High point (1760 m). Descend gradually to west.

2.8 — Washout on terrace (1725 m). At low water, descend to west and proceed to next headland; otherwise, detour to left for 600 metres on narrow path through trees.

3.2 — Rejoin old jeep track briefly before descending onto flat. Follow faint bulldozed swath rising gradually to west.

6.9 — Trail fades; follow cairns.

7.2 — End of trail (1790 m) at shallow lake at toe of Saskatchewan Glacier. The glacier is not readily accessible from this point because of steep and unstable ice-cored moraine.

This hike toward the toe of the Saskatchewan Glacier gives an appreciation of the effects of glaciation, past and present. This glacier is the longest of the six principal tongues flowing down from the Columbia Icefield.

Starting at an old bridge over a deep, narrow gorge of the North Saskatchewan River (of which this glacier is the source), the most direct trail turns right immediately and follows above the river. More distance can be saved by taking an old track across the gravel flats before the wooded hill ahead.

An old jeep road, constructed for military training purposes, winds up the hill, staying clear of a chasm on the river. Dropping down on the other side of the knoll sees arrival at unexpectedly wide flats.

Some 12,000 years ago this valley was filled by a glacier perhaps 300 metres deep; more recently, the Little Ice Age advance of the late 1800s left its mark in the trim lines (below which no vegetation has become established) on the valley walls near the toe.

From the flats, there are views of Mt. Athabasca and the icefalls (cont. p. 140)

Toe of Saskatchewan Glacier and ridge of Mt. Andromeda from near end of *Saskatchewan Glacier Toe* trail.

(cont. from p. 139) on the southeastern side of Mt. Andromeda. The toe of the Saskatchewan Glacier soon comes into sight, but it's father away than it appears. Eventually reach the end of the trail shortly before the opaque lake at the toe.

Mountaineers gain access to the glacier by crossing the outlet stream on a log-jam at the head of the gorge near the start of this trail. Of course, glacier travel requires the proper knowledge and equipment. It's also recommended to take out voluntary safety registration (see p. 15).

It is possible to make out people on the *Parker Ridge* trail up to the north from this outing. Taking that trail gives a fine overall view of the Saskatchewan Glacier, whereas this one grants an intriguing ice-level perspective.

Old "Wonder Trail"

Distance: 1.7 km (1.1 mi) — Icefields Parkway to Nigel Creek
Walk: 20—30 minutes one way
Elevation loss: 55 m (180 ft)
Maximum elevation: 1645 m (5395 ft)
Maps: Gem Trek 1:75,000 Columbia Icefield and NTS 1:50,000 Columbia Icefield 83 C/3
Trailhead: As for *Saskatchewan Glacier Toe* trail (see p. 139).

0.0 — Old bridge (elevation 1645 m) over gorge on North Saskatchewan River. Follow old road to south, descending gradually; *Saskatchewan Glacier Toe* trail veers to right immediately south of bridge.
0.3 — Keep straight; old jeep track (alternate route to toe of Saskatchewan Glacier) to right.
0.6 — Keep straight; path down to creek to right.
1.1 — Cross old bridge over gorge.
1.7 — Old bridge over Nigel Creek (1590 m). Nigel Falls upstream.

This short walk follows a section of the old route between Lake Louise and Jasper, known to early travellers as the "Wonder Trail."

Head downhill from the 1939 bridge over the North Saskatchewan River; looking over the railing reveals the little-known feature of a deep, narrow gorge just upstream.

Keeping straight past the junction with the old track that leads toward the Saskatchewan Glacier and descend a wide switchback. At an old pulloff on the right, a short, steep path leads down to the stream. Here water cascades over rock steps on its descent from the glaciers on the north face of Mt. Saskatchewan.

Continuing on the old road, a wooden bridge leads over the gorge of the North Saskatchewan again, then the trail traverses an open, south-facing slope. Arriving at a third bridge, this one over Nigel Creek, the present highway is high above. If the water level is low enough for safety, it is possible to venture upstream in the creek-bed for a view of Nigel Falls. This sight is missed by highway travellers, because the falls are practically under the bridge and thus not visible from it.

The old road continues farther southeast, joining the Icefields Parkway in another 1.5 km, at the base of the long upgrade to the modern crossing of Nigel Creek.

Note that this is not considered a formal trail and is not maintained, so that the bridges are not examined for safety. As of May, 2001, the bridges show signs of age but are passable with care. Bears use this old road.

Panther Falls, Nigel Creek

Distance: 1.0 km (0.6 mi) — Icefields Parkway to Panther Falls viewpoint
Walk: 15—20 minutes one way
Elevation loss: 35 m (115 ft)
Maximum elevation: 1790 m (5870 ft)
Maps: Gem Trek 1:75,000 Columbia Icefield and NTS 1:50,000 Columbia Icefield 83 C/3
Trailhead: Parking area on east side of Icefields Parkway, 2.0 km (1.2 mi) north of the parking area on the Big Bend and 0.9 km (0.6 mi) south of entrance to parking area for *Nigel Creek* trail.

0.0 — Southeast corner of parking area (elevation 1790 m). Descend switchbacks.
1.0 — Panther Falls viewpoint (1755 m).

This short trail gives a view of the full extent of Panther Falls tumbling over a 55 metre drop on Nigel Creek. (Caution: Stay clear of the dangerous edge at the lip of the falls, close to the highway.)

Panther Falls were named in 1907 by Mary Schäffer because a cougar followed her party along the trail nearby.

The falls are particularly beautiful when sun sparkling on the mist creates a shimmering rainbow; the best time to see this, and the best lighting for photography, is in the morning.

Nigel Creek with Nigel Pass to right.

Nigel Pass

Distance: 7.3 km (4.5 mi) — Icefields Parkway to Nigel Pass
Day hike/backpack: 2.5—3 hours one way
Elevation loss: 10 m (33 ft)
Elevation gain: 375 m (1230 ft)
Maximum elevation: 2205 m (7230 ft)
Maps: Gem Trek 1:75,000 Columbia Icefield and NTS 1:50,000 Columbia Icefield 83 C/3
Trailhead: Parking area on east side of Icefields Parkway, 0.9 km (0.6 mi) north of parking area for *Panther Falls* trail and 4.3 km (2.7 mi) south of parking area for *Parker Ridge* trail.

0.0 — Gate (elevation 1840 m) at north end of parking area. Head down old road.

0.1 — Sign (1830 m). Turn right off old road and cross footbridge over Nigel Creek. Work up east side of creek, passing through several avalanche paths.

2.2 — Site of former Camp Parker. Head north up valley of Nigel Creek, ascending steadily.

5.2 — Emerge into subalpine meadows; veer away from drainage and climb more steeply.

7.3 — Nigel Pass (2205 m) and Banff/Jasper national parks boundary. Trail continues northwest, descending into valley of Brazeau River in Jasper National Park.

Nigel Pass, at the northern end of Banff National Park, is often traversed by backpackers heading into neighbouring Jasper National Park, yet even a day hike there shows that the Banff side of the pass has attractions of its own. After (cont. p. 144)

Cascades on north tributary of Nigel Creek.

(cont. from p. 143) passing through several large slidepaths, in just over 2 km reach the site of Camp Parker: a base for pioneering parties of backcountry travellers. Nowadays, however, it is not permitted to stay overnight anywhere along this trail.

A variety of brightly-coloured wildflowers flourish in the meadows at the head of this trail. As well, there is a view back to the south over Parker Ridge toward Mt. Saskatchewan, with its distinct strata, plus a glimpse of the Hilda Glacier east of Mt. Athabasca. An option from Nigel Pass is to head southeast up to steep, rocky Cataract Pass and drop into the White Goat Wilderness Area.

An alternative to the established trail through Nigel Pass presents itself in a path that can be picked up on the west side of the northwest branch of Nigel Creek. Reach a small lake in about 1.7 km, then continue another 400 metres to the edge of a steep drop-off. This is the true low point of Nigel Pass, with an excellent view into the upper reaches of the Brazeau Valley in Jasper National Park. (A steep, rocky path descends there, as does the main trail.)

Yet another possibility in this area is an exploratory jaunt up the valley to the northwest, at the head of which lies the most northerly point in Banff National Park. It is better to stay high to the north at the start, since heading up the drainage leads into a narrow notch whose passage involves considerable bushwhacking. Once at the first flats on this tributary, it is more straightforward to follow upstream. A small gorge with impressive cascades can be easily skirted, then reach open country with freedom to choose whatever route wished.

Always to the left is the sheer cliffband along the eastern aspect of Nigel Peak: this formidable barrier is breached only by two waterfalls from lakes above on a bench. If using the NTS 1:50,000 scale maps, the Sunwapta Peak sheet (code 83 C/6) is needed to navigate to the Banff/Jasper national parks boundary.

The name associated with the pass, peak, and creek comes from Nigel Vavasour, guide to exploratory mountaineers J.N. Collie and H.E.M. Stutfield on their 1897 trip to this area.

Saskatchewan Glacier and Castleguard Mountain from end of *Parker Ridge* trail.

Parker Ridge

Distance: 2.4 km (1.5 mi) — Icefields Parkway to Saskatchewan Glacier viewpoint
Day hike: 45 minutes—1 hour one way
Elevation gain: 270 m (885 ft)
Elevation loss: 20 m (65 ft)
Maximum elevation: 2280 m (7480 ft)
Maps: Gem Trek 1:75,000 Columbia Icefield and NTS 1:50,000 Columbia Icefield 83 C/3
Trailhead: Parking area on south side of Icefields Parkway, 4.3 km (2.7 mi) north of the Nigel Creek parking area and 4.2 km (2.6 mi) south of the Banff/Jasper national parks boundary at Sunwapta Pass.

0.0 — Sign (elevation 2010 m). Climb steadily—stay on switchbacks to avoid eroding trail and trampling vegetation.
1.9 — Crest (2280 m) of saddle on Parker Ridge. Descend gradually to southeast.
2.4 — End of trail (2260 m) and Saskatchewan Glacier viewpoint.

This trail is often closed early in the season to protect soggy ground from trampling. (Alternatives in the area include the *Old "Wonder Trail," Nigel Pass, Hilda Glacier,* and *Boundary Lake* trails.) When this *Parker Ridge* trail is open, the switch-backing ascent up to alpine terrain is one of the most rewarding short hikes in Banff National Park.

The trail passes through scattered stands of stunted subalpine fir. Wildflowers such as white mountain heather are adapted to the harsh conditions here, and thrive despite wind, cold, and high ultraviolet radiation. Mountain goats might be seen feeding on the sparse vegetation in the vicinity; grizzly bears also frequent Parker Ridge.

A superlative view of the entire length of the Saskatchewan Glacier awaits at the end of the trail. This is the longest of the six outlet valley glaciers that radiate from the Columbia Icefield. Mt. Castleguard rises in the distance above the glacier; the summit block of Mt. Athabasca and attendant towers appear like obelisks to the west.

It's also possible to gaze some distance down the North Saskatchewan River, which has a long journey from its icy source.

Hilda Glacier

Distance: 1.4 km (0.9 mi) — Icefields Parkway to terminal moraine of Hilda Glacier
Day hike: 20—30 minutes one way
Elevation gain: 180 m (590 ft)
Maximum elevation: 2195 m (7200 ft)
Maps: Gem Trek 1:75,000 Columbia Icefield and NTS 1:50,000 Columbia Icefield 83 C/3
Trailhead: Parking area on east side of Icefields Parkway, 0.3 km (0.2 mi) north of Hilda Creek youth hostel service road and 3.0 km (1.9 mi) south of Banff/Jasper national parks boundary in Sunwapta Pass.

0.0 — West side of highway opposite trailhead (elevation 2015 m). Descend slightly into drainage and pick up faint path along north side of Hilda Creek.
1.0 — Terminal moraine of Hilda Glacier. Climb to north of lateral moraine.
1.4 — End of path on crest of lateral moraine (2195 m).

This is an interesting short outing from near the Hilda Creek Hostel. There is a faint path along the north side of the creek; the trail disappears on the crest of the north lateral moraine of the glacier.

A scrambling route can be made beyond trail's end to travel over undulating piles of rocky material carried down by ice. There might be a cave at the toe of the glacier: keep in mind that its ceiling may be unstable and that the level of any water in it could suddenly change. Don't try to walk on the heavily crevassed glacier.

Looking up at the looming east face of Mt. Athabasca, it is impressive to realize that it has been ascended. It is also apparent why the standard mountaineering route to the summit does not head up here. (It goes via the north glacier, which is still a demanding approach that calls for ice axe, rope, harness, helmet, and crampons.)

Ice cave at toe of Hilda Glacier.

Boundary Lake

Distance: 1.5 km (0.9 mi) — Icefields Parkway to west end of Boundary Lake
Day hike: 20—30 minutes one way
Elevation loss: 5 m (16 ft)
Elevation gain: 60 m (195 ft)
Maximum elevation: 2080 m (6820 ft)
Maps: Gem Trek 1:75,000 Columbia Icefield and NTS 1:50,000 Columbia Icefield 83 C/3
Trailhead: Parking area on west side of Icefields Parkway at Banff/Jasper national parks boundary in Sunwapta Pass.

0.0 — Northwest corner of parking area (elevation 2025 m). Take path down to west.
0.1 — Turn left along old roadway (2020 m).
0.5 — Turn right off roadway and climb beside drainage.
1.1 — East end of Boundary Lake. Follow along south shore.
1.5 — West end of Boundary Lake (2080 m).

This short outing leads to a hidden lake near the Banff/Jasper boundary at Sunwapta Pass, so it can serve as an introduction or a farewell to Banff National Park.

It is possible to continue off-trail beyond the west end of the lake toward the toe of the steep Boundary Glacier that rumbles down from the northeast face of Mt. Athabasca.

On the return are views to the east, where the grey spires of Nigel Peak form a jagged horizon.

Golden-mantled ground squirrel.

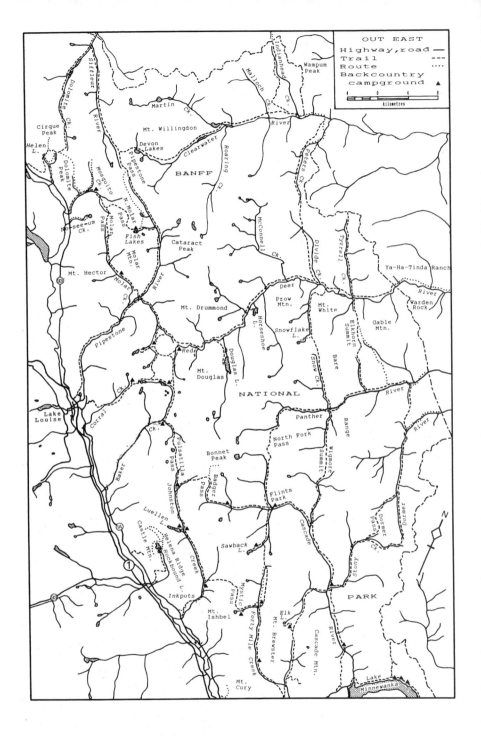

Out East

Wampum Peak from *Indianhead Creek* trail.

Forty Mile Creek

Distance: 27.8 km (17.2 mi) — *Cascade Amphitheatre* trail to Flints Park
Backpack: 1.5—2 days one way
Elevation gain: 600 m (1970 ft)
Elevation loss: 460 m (1510 ft)
Maximum elevation: 2150 m (7050 ft)
Maps: Gem Trek 1:100,000 Banff & Mt. Assiniboine, and NTS 1:50,000 Banff 82-O/4 and Castle Mountain 82-O/5
Trailhead: Km 0.7 of *Cascade Amphitheatre* trail (see p. 52).

0.0 — Sign (elevation 1680 m). Turn left; straight ahead leads toward Cascade Amphitheatre. Cross a series of ski runs and enter forest, climbing steadily.

1.7 — High point (1750 m). Descend to Forty Mile Creek.

3.3 — Keep straight over footbridge (1620 m) to north side of creek; connector from *Cascade Amphitheatre* trail comes in on right.

5.3 — Keep straight; *Edith Pass* trail to left. Trail follows gradual bend of Forty Mile Creek to head north.

7.5 — Backcountry campground.

12.8 — Keep right; outfitter's camps to left.

15.2 — Keep straight (1835 m); *Mystic Pass* trail to left.

15.4 — Turn right on hiker trail; horse trail keeps straight. Backcountry campground and junction with connector to *Mystic Pass* trail 100 metres along horse trail.

20.6 — Hiker trail rejoins horse trail.

21.2 — Forty Mile Summit (2150 m). Continue north through meadows.

22.9 — Keep straight; Rainbow Lake 1.0 km to east. Trail begins steeper descent and veers west.

24.2 — Turn right after crossing creek; trail to left leads to backcountry campground (1.4 km) and Sawback Lake (2.2 km). Follow downstream above Sawback Creek on west side.

27.0 — Reach south edge of meadows in valley of Cascade River.

27.7 — Cross footbridge over Cascade River.

27.8 — Flints Park junction (1820 m) and end of *Flints Park* trail at km 8.1. *North Cascade River* trail to north; *Badger Pass* trail to west. Warden cabin 50 metres east.

Most of the valley of Forty Mile Creek is forested and thus a long haul with few views, though occasionally there are glimpses of the east side of the Sawback Range.

Mts. Edith and Louis are prominent; Mt. Fifi is equally spectacular yet unduly ignored because of its more famous neighbours. (Its incongruous name doesn't help its cause, bringing to mind a poodle all shorn and trimmed like some hedge decoration—it *was* apparently named after a dog.)

Cross several avalanche paths as working up the valley and pass the junction with the *Mystic Pass* trail, then begin a steeper climb toward Forty Mile Summit. Don't forget to look back south from the top of the pass to take in the larch-framed panora-

South from Forty Mile Summit to peaks of Sawback Range including prominent Mt. Louis.

ma of peaks.

On the north side of Forty Mile Summit, Sawback Lake deserves a visit. Beavers have penetrated this high, remote valley to colonize the meadows below the lake. The backcountry campground situated on a treed ridge in the middle of the meadows makes for a good overnight stop (or, using the bearproof storage cables, a safe place to leave a pack if simply making a side trip to Sawback Lake). Rugged peaks of the Sawback Range surround the lake; to the east stand the steep limestone slabs of the Brewster massif.

The final stretch of the *Forty Mile Creek* trail, which runs from Sawback Lake above Sawback Creek down to Flints Park, is frequented by grizzly bears.

Mystic Pass

Distance: 13.4 km (8.3 mi) — *Forty Mile Creek* trail to *Johnston Creek* trail
Backpack: 4—5 hours one way
Elevation gain: 430 m (1410 ft)
Elevation loss: 595 m (1950 ft)
Maximum elevation: 2270 m (7445 ft)
Maps: Gem Trek 1:100,000 Banff & Mt. Assiniboine and NTS 1:50,000 Castle Mountain 82-O/5
Trailhead: Km 15.2 of *Forty Mile Creek* trail (see p. 150).

0.0 — Sign (elevation 1835 m). Head west; *Forty Mile Creek* trail to north.
0.1 — Cross footbridge over Forty Mile Creek.
0.2 — Turn right to travel along fence of warden cabin corral and past junction with connector from *Forty Mile Creek* trail. Climb steadily.
2.7 — Backcountry campground.
3.2 — Keep right; Mystic Lake 500 metres to left. Climb steeply.
6.8 — Mystic Pass (2270 m). Descend steeply to west.
13.4 — Junction (1675 m) with *Johnston Creek* trail at km 2.1.

The name Mystic Pass evokes an alluring spell. Heeding the siren call, take this trail to visit it. Below the pass, Mystic Lake shelters in a high, larch-embroidered valley beneath the eastern ramparts of Mt. Ishbel.

Mystic Lake.

Mystic Pass, with 2530 m ridge in distance.

A path encircles Mystic Lake, allowing the surrounding vistas to be taken in from different angles. To get an unusual perspective upon the lake if doing this trail in the opposite direction to the description, stay high after Mystic Pass and contour south for about 1.5 km, passing above a tiny tarn, to a small saddle in a ridge.

This lofty perch some 275 metres above the lake grants a bird's-eye view; then sidle down an open slope to reach the water (perhaps doing some boot-skiing on late-lying avalanche snow).

An interesting excursion from Mystic Pass, if have energy to spare after reaching its 2270 m height, is to take a steep but well-defined game trail up to the ridge marking the divide with Forty Mile Creek. Gaining its crest reveals a sheer drop to the east, with the serrated summits of the Vermilion Range across the valley and two small lakes almost directly below.

A short scramble up to a knoll about 300 metres northwest takes in the sweep of the narrow valley leading down toward Johnston Creek. Beyond to the west rise Helena Ridge and the summit of Castle Mountain, both also visible from the main trail.

Past these, however, from this vantage point at approximately 2530 m, can be seen Boom Mountain, Storm Mountain, and—across the continental divide—Kootenay National Park in British Columbia. A further bonus is the sight of the sharp silhouettes of the Sawback Range to the south.

A fine three-day, two-night trip is up Forty Mile Creek, over Mystic Pass, down steadily to Johnston Creek, and out to the Bow Valley Parkway via the Ink Pots. A longer loop can be made via Badger Pass.

Muleshoe

Distance: 1.1 km (0.7 mi) — Bow Valley Parkway to Muleshoe viewpoint
Walk: 20—30 minutes one way
Elevation gain: 65 m (215 ft)
Maximum elevation: 1465 m (4805 ft)
Maps: Gem Trek 1:100,000 Banff & Mt. Assiniboine and NTS 1:50,000 Banff 82-O/4
Trailhead: Parking area for picnic tables on the west side of the Bow Valley Parkway (Highway 1A), 5.5 km (3.4 mi) north of its southern end at the Trans-Canada Highway and 12.0 km (7.4 mi) south of the Johnston Canyon parking area. **Note:** The Bow Valley Parkway is closed between Fireside picnic area and Johnston Canyon from 6 p.m. to 9 a.m., March 1st to June 25th.

0.0 — Sign (elevation 1400 m) above east side of highway opposite picnic area. Climb, mostly gradually, on narrow path through grove of trembling aspen and into coniferous forest.
1.1 — Viewpoint (1465 m) at base of grassy slope.

This short jaunt leads through stands of trembling aspen and conifers (regenerating after a prescribed burn) to a viewpoint over the Bow Valley. Here can be seen the marshy area known as Backswamp and the ox-bow lakes created when bends in the Bow River were cut off by the creation of new, more direct channels.

Energetic hikers can push up the very steep slope above the viewpoint for progressively more expansive panoramas (see p. 5), including north to Castle Mountain and to Mt. Temple near Lake Louise. Wildflower aficionados will enjoy the spectacle of paintbrush, harebell, shrubby cinquefoil, wild gaillardia (brown-eyed Susan), golden rattle, yarrow, and many other species splashing their colours over the meadows.

For the truly ambitious, a faint path leads up around the head of the grassy slope to the north and then heads up a steep ridge where mountain goats might be sighted. This outlier of Mt. Cory tops out at over 2250 m. While resting from the exertion needed to get there, the surroundings can be contemplated—a highlight is the soaring pinnacle known as The Finger, named by pioneer climber Lawrence Grassi (who led the first ascent).

Species of flora that can be observed during this scramble include prairie crocus, spotted saxifrage, forget-me-not, and larkspur. Near the top of the ridge are whitebark pines, on the seeds of which Clark's nutcrackers feed.

Bow River from extension to *Muleshoe* trail.

Pilot Pond

Distance: 0.2. km (0.1 mi) — Bow Valley Parkway to Pilot Pond
Walk: 5—10 minutes one way
Elevation loss: 10 m (33 ft)
Maximum elevation: 1430 m (4690 ft)
Maps: Gem Trek 1:100,000 Banff & Mt. Assiniboine and NTS 1:50,000 Banff 82-O/4
Trailhead: Parking area on west side of one-way southbound lane of Bow Valley Parkway (Highway 1A), 2.3 km (1.4 mi) south of Johnston Canyon. **Note:** The Bow Valley Parkway is closed between Fireside picnic area and Johnston Canyon from 6 p.m. to 9 a.m., March 1st to June 25th.

0.0 — Sign (elevation 1430 m). Descend to west.
0.2 — North end of Pilot Lake (1420 m). A 1.0 km path circumnavigates this small body of water.

This very short stroll leads to a small lake off the Bow Valley Parkway. Its main attraction used to be to anglers, but winter-kill in 1990-1991 saw the end of the non-native fish that had been stocked there.

Now—as documented by Mike and Diane McIvor of Banff in their amphibian survey—the long-toed salamanders that gave it the earlier name of Lizard Lake are once again found here. One of only two species of salamander in Alberta, they have limited distribution in Banff National Park. The disappearance of the fish, which preyed on larval salamanders and ate the zooplankton that the adults need, seems to have enabled the salamanders (which live three to five years) to make a comeback.

The present name of the pond comes from Pilot Mountain to the south across the Bow Valley, which was itself named since its distinctive flat-topped summit served as a navigational landmark for early travellers.

Blue grouse.

Johnston Canyon/Ink Pots

Distance: 5.9 km (3.7 mi) — Bow Valley Parkway to the Ink Pots
Walk/day hike: 1.5—2 hours one way
Elevation gain: 335 m (1100 ft)
Elevation loss: 115 m (375 ft)
Maximum elevation: 1760 m (5775 ft)
Maps: Gem Trek 1:100,000 Banff & Mt. Assiniboine, and NTS 1:50,000 Banff 82-O/4 and Castle Mountain 82-O/5
Trailhead: Parking area on east side of Bow Valley Parkway (Highway 1A), south of bridge over Johnston Creek and entrance to Johnston Canyon Resort; 12.0 km (7.4 mi) north of the entrance to the Muleshoe picnic area and 6.5 km (4.0 mi) south of Castle Junction. **Note:** The Bow Valley Parkway is closed between Fireside picnic area and Johnston Canyon from 6 p.m. to 9 a.m., March 1st to June 25th. (Trailhead access during these times is possible via the Trans-Canada Highway, turning off to travel south on Highway 1A from Castle Junction.)

0.0 — Trailhead kiosk (elevation 1425 m) in northeast corner of parking area. Take paved path past washrooms.

0.1 — Cross Johnston Creek on footbridge and turn right.

0.2 — Keep straight; hard left is Johnston Canyon Resort. Travel through canyon, in places on catwalk suspended above creek.

1.2 — Turn up left on switchbacking steps; Lower Falls 50 metres straight ahead (viewpoint, footbridge over creek, tunnel for close view). Continue up canyon.

2.6 — Keep left at top of steps after viewpoint; to right leads to lower viewpoint of Upper Falls in 100 metres.

2.7 — Upper viewpoint of Upper Falls. Continue on gravel trail beyond railing above falls.

3.2 — Keep right on old road; left leads to Moose Meadows parking area on Bow Valley Parkway in 2.7 km.

4.5 — High point (1760 m).

5.9 — The Ink Pots (1645 m).

Upper Falls on *Johnston Canyon/Ink Pots* trail, from lower viewpoint.

Backpacker at one of the Ink Pots, with reflection of Mt. Ishbel.

This very popular trail, in places suspended high above the gorge, leads through the deep narrow slot down which Johnston Creek flows. Interpretive signs along the first part of the trail elaborate upon the geological history of the canyon.

The Lower Falls, a mere 1.2 km from the trailhead, plunge over a lip into a large pool, of which there are dramatic views thanks to a bridge. This bridge leads to a tunnel whose far end is close to the top of the falls...expect to be greeted by spray!

Small, plump, dark grey birds are likely to be seen along the creek: these are American dippers, intriguing inhabitants of mountain streams that nest in mossy domes attached to sheer cliffs near waterfalls. Dippers often bob up and down (hence the name), have a melodious song given even in the depths of winter [they are year-round residents], use their wings to swim underwater, and have specially evolved feet that allow them to walk on streambottoms. {The last two adaptations help in their pursuit of larvae and small fish.}

Another interesting bird species that breeds in Johnston Canyon is the black swift, usually seen returning late on summer evenings from a day of capturing insects to feed its young. This is one of only two nesting colonies that have been identified in Alberta (the other is at Maligne Canyon in Jasper National Park). The number of active nests in Johnston Canyon is usually five to ten; each pair raises but one young per year.

The Upper Falls, higher than the Lower Falls, can be viewed from both above and below; rainbows often arc through the mist. The lower viewpoint is the best place to see the tall columns of brown mineral deposits that drape the canyon walls.

Continuing beyond the paved trail, join a wide, steep trail that climbs to a crest with glimpses of the creek far below. The final section of the trail is downhill to the Ink Pots, a collection of seven small, clear, circular springs in a meadow above Johnston Creek. These are karst features, caused by solution of limestone; the source of the water is unknown.

Johnston Creek

Distance: 20.0 km (12.4 mi) — Ink Pots to Pulsatilla Pass
Backpack: 1.5—2 days one way
Elevation gain: 710 m (2330 ft)
Maximum elevation: 2355 m (7725 ft)
Maps: Gem Trek 1:100,000 Banff & Mt. Assiniboine and NTS 1:50,000 Castle Mountain 82-O/5
Trailhead: End of *Johnston Canyon/Ink Pots* trail at km 5.9 (see p. 156).

0.0 — Sign (elevation 1645 m). Continue northeast across meadows beyond Ink Pots.

0.3 — Cross footbridge to east side of Johnston Creek.

0.4 — Keep straight; former Hillsdale trail to right no longer maintained.

2.0 — Backcountry campground.

2.1 — Cross footbridge and keep straight; *Mystic Pass* trail to right.

5.8 — Pass warden cabin.

10.6 — Keep straight; to left leads to backcountry campground and footbridge over Johnston Creek in 200 metres, and east end of Luellen Lake and another backcountry campground in 1. 2 km.

11.1 — Footbridge to west side of Johnston Creek.

12.2 — Footbridge to east side of Johnston Creek.

16.1 — Keep straight (2025 m); *Badger Pass* trail to right.

16.6 — Backcountry campground to left of trail.

20.0 — Pulsatilla Pass (2355 m). Trail to north descends Wildflower Creek to Baker Creek (see the author's *Hiking Lake Louise*, Luminous Compositions).

Part of Helena Ridge (left) and Stuart Knob (centre) from east end of Luellen Lake.

Up Johnston Creek from uppermost footbridge.

Much of the way up Johnston Creek from the Ink Pots is through forest with limited views, but an attraction of this long trail is its guarantee of a wilderness experience.

Occasional avalanche paths give views west toward Helena Ridge; a closer sight of its steep cliffs is possible by taking the short side trip to Luellen Lake. The backcountry campground at the east end of the lake is a popular base for backcountry anglers. It also reveals Stuart Knob above the rockbands at the far end of the lake.

Continuing up Johnston Creek, break into meadows that allow views of the surrounding mountains. There may be some confusion as a result of two parallel trails in this upper section: it's best to stay to the east. Beyond the Badger Pass junction, rise—steeply near the end—through subalpine larches to Pulsatilla Pass. En route, catch views of a hanging glacier on the east face of Pulsatilla Mountain.

Pulsatilla was once the scientific name for a genus of the buttercup family, of which western anemone is a member. Its large, creamy white flowers adorn the alpine zone throughout Banff National Park.

Badger Pass

Distance: 17.5 km (10.9 mi) — *Johnston Creek* trail to *Flints Park* trail
Backpack: 4.5—5.5 hours one way
Elevation gain: 515 m (1690 ft)
Elevation loss: 720 m (2360 ft)
Maximum elevation: 2540 m (8330 ft)
Maps: Gem Trek 1:100,000 Banff & Mt. Assiniboine and NTS 1:50,000 Castle Mountain 82-O/5
Trailhead: Km 16.1 of *Johnston Creek* trail (see p. 158).

0.0 — Sign (elevation 2025 m). Head northeast up drainage, climbing steadily.

5.0 — Badger Pass (2540 m). **Note:** This pass is often blocked by snow well into summer. Turn right to descend steeply to south toward Cascade River.

8.5 — Trail levels out and veers east down Cascade Valley.

12.0 — Cross creek [possible rudimentary two-log footbridge] to backcountry campground. Path toward cliff below Block Lakes (technical climbing) leaves on opposite side of river. Main trail continues east through wide meadows.

17.3 — Keep straight; wide track to left connects with *North Cascade River* trail at km 0.2.

17.5 — Junction (1820 m) at end of *Flints Park* trail. Straight ahead leads to *Upper Cascade Valley* trail, to right is *Forty Mile Creek* trail, and to left is *North Cascade River* trail.

Snowdrift in Badger Pass, late July.

West from summit of South Bonnet Peak to mountains of the continental divide near Lake Louise.

Climbing steeply from Johnston Creek, this trail leads to one of the highest points that can be reached on an established, maintained trail in Banff National Park.

Passing through meadows and a few subalpine larches, eventually negotiate a low headwall and steadily ascend the last grade to Badger Pass. The name seems to be a misnomer since it is unlikely that one of those animals ever made it to this alpine setting; perhaps the "badger" was a hoary marmot.

A snowdrift, which may be corniced, often lingers here well into summer, so check at a park visitor centre to determine whether the trail is open.

If have lots of energy left after reaching Badger Pass, consider going up South Bonnet Peak. The ascent follows a straightforward line up to a saddle at the south edge of the extensive Bonnet Glacier, then over the scree of the west ridge past a false summit to a large cairn. The elevation of 3215 m (10,545 ft) grants a superb panorama: the landmark peaks in sight stretch from Mt. Assiniboine in the south to Mt. Forbes in the north.

The top, first reached by surveyor A. St. Cyr in 1890, also reveals Douglas Lake and the mysterious-sounding Valley of the Hidden Lakes. This rarely seen part of the park is accessible from the *Red Deer River* trail.

The usual course from Badger Pass is to descend steeply into the drainage of the Cascade River. Upon reaching the main valley, turn east toward Flints Park. At first the trail is a rough one through forest; after the backcountry campground at km 12.0 it levels out in open meadows.

A side trail leads from near the backcountry campground to the base of the cliff below the Block Lakes, where an old black-and-white sign indicates the line through the rockband. However, most parties that attempt this route do so roped up.

161

Rockbound Lake

Distance: 8.4 km (5.2 mi) — Bow Valley Parkway to Rockbound Lake
Day hike: 2.5—3 hours one way
Elevation gain: 760 m (2495 ft)
Maximum elevation: 2210 m (7250 ft)
Maps: Gem Trek 1:100,000 Banff & Mt. Assiniboine and NTS 1:50,000 Castle Mountain 82-O/5
Trailhead: Parking area on north side of Bow Valley Parkway, 6.5 km (4.0 mi) west of Johnston Canyon and 0.2 km (0.1 mi) east of the intersection of connector from Trans-Canada Highway with the Bow Valley Parkway at Castle Junction.

0.0 — Trailhead kiosk (elevation 1450 m). Head north through forest.
0.3 — Keep straight; *Silverton Falls* trail to right. Climb steadily.
5.0 — Trail narrows and turns northwest after passing around ridge of Castle Mountain. Continue climbing, although more gradually; some boggy sections.
7.7 — Tower Lake. Trail continues from northeast corner of lake, climbing steep switchbacks through cliffband.
8.4 — Rockbound Lake (2210 m).

The author at Rockbound Lake.

Sweet coltsfoot.

The hike to Rockbound Lake is relentlessly steep, but the destination is deserving of the demands it puts on legs and lungs. The first subalpine larches occur just before small Tower Lake.

A short but steep trail leads through the headwall beyond Tower Lake to Rockbound Lake, which is indeed surrounded on its west, north, and east sides by sheer limestone walls. Osprey may be sighted here, looking for fish in the clear, deep blue water. (This bird was on the back of $10 bills before a new design in 2001.)

It is possible, with a bit of scrambling, to circumnavigate the lake. En route there is a peninsula, jutting out from the west shore, that is difficult to distinguish from the south shore where the trail arrives at Rockbound Lake. Look for sweet coltsfoot blooming here early in the season.

Silverton Falls

Distance: 0.8 km (0.5 mi) — *Rockbound Lake* trail to Silverton Falls viewpoint
Walk: 20—30 minutes one way
Elevation gain: 65 m (215 ft)
Maximum elevation: 1515 m (4970 ft)
Maps: Gem Trek 1:100,000 Banff & Mt. Assiniboine and NTS 1:50,000 Castle Mountain 82-O/5
Trailhead: Km 0.3 of *Rockbound Lake* trail (see p. 162).

0.0 — Sign (elevation 1450 m). Turn right off *Rockbound Lake* trail.
0.5 — Turn hard left (former footbridge crossed creek).
0.8 — Silverton Falls viewpoint (1515 m).

     This short outing off the *Rockbound Lake* trail reveals impressive falls on Silverton Creek, which drains Rockbound and Tower lakes. Switchbacks on the west side end at a viewpoint for the high waterfall dropping in two punchbowl-like sections through a tight rocky chasm.

     A bonus on the return is the view west across the Bow Valley to Storm Mountain.

**Upper portion of
Silverton Falls.**

Castle Mountain/Helena Ridge

Distance: Approx. 5.7 km (3.5 mi) — Suggested route to true summit of Castle Mountain
Off-trail scramble: 2—2.5 hours one way
Elevation gain: 870 m (2855 ft)
Elevation loss: 230 m (755 ft)
Maximum elevation: 2880 m (9450 ft)
Maps: Gem Trek 1:100,000 Banff & Mt. Assiniboine and NTS 1:50,000 Castle Mountain 82-O/5
Trailhead: End of *Rockbound Lake* trail at km 8.4 (see p. 162).

0.0 — End of *Rockbound Lake* trail on southeast shore (elevation 2210 m). Head right and follow along water's edge, going around east cove and angling up to gully in cliffband.

0.8 — Take gully up through cliffband (cairns at top). Turn north on well-defined trail up knoll.

1.2 — Unmarked intersection: this route continues north up to symmetrical peak at north end of Helena Ridge; this is also where rejoin the outbound route on the return from the true summit of Castle Mountain. (In addition, this is where veer west in a wide sweeping traverse of approx. 2.5 km to the high point—elevation 2766 m (9070 ft)—at the south end of Castle Mountain.)

1.8 — Saddle southeast of symmetrical peak at north end of Helena Ridge.

2.3 — North peak of Helena Ridge (2880 m). Descend west to wide gradual ridge leading to Stuart Knob.

3.7 — Low point on ridge (2650 m). Ascend toward Stuart Knob, passing below its southeast face.

4.7 — Gain ridge (2785 m) to west of summit block of Stuart Knob; to reach its top—elevation 2820 m (9250 ft)—approach via northwest aspect. For true summit of Castle Mountain, proceed southwest, turning west for last 300 metres.

5.7 — True summit of Castle Mountain (2850 m). To return to km 1.2 intersection, retrace steps toward Stuart Knob, then descend southeast from ridge.

Off-trail scrambling enthusiasts can explore at will in the alpine terrain above Rockbound Lake. Access to the high open country above the lake is via a notch in the cliffband above the east shore. Beyond the gap a section of trail, visible from below, leads up to a knoll.

From this point there's free rein. Among the options is a full-day jaunt beginning with the climb to the top of the symmetrical cone at the northwest end of Helena Ridge. From there, descend west to and cruise along the wide, usually windy ridge, on which—despite the exposed conditions—grow flowers such as bladder campion and inflated oxytrope. This leads to the base of Stuart Knob, whose isolated summit block, most easily ascended from the north, surprises with a view of Luellen Lake to the east over 800 metres below.

To continue to the true summit of Castle Mountain, head southwest, noting that the final ridge to the top can be dangerously corniced—stay well (cont. p. 166) (cont. from p. 165) back from the edge. The top gives a heart-pounding appreciation of the virtually vertical west face of Castle Mountain, and takes in a veritable sea of peaks. A particularly interesting portion of the panorama is that upon the hanging glacier on Bident Mountain and Mt. Quadra west across the Bow Valley.

Among other possibilities from Rockbound Lake is the ascent of the highest point at the south end of Castle Mountain. Contour southwest above the cliffs that encircle the lake, then climb south toward the highest of the four blocks on the skyline. An easy final approach is from the west via a gully.

The elevation of 2766 m (9072 ft) does not place this peak among the giants of the Rockies, but there are impressive views nevertheless, as well as the satisfaction of experiencing this well-known feature of Banff National Park in an unusual manner.

The name of Castle Mountain, aptly given by Sir James Hector in 1858, has gone through changes over the years. It was altered to Mt. Eisenhower in 1946, in honour of the Second World War general. However, public sentiment in favour of the original name of this striking landmark led to its reinstatement in 1979. (With typical Canadian compromise and tact, the high buttress at the southeast end is known as Eisenhower Peak.)

Unusual dome formation on Castle Mountain highlighted by snow, viewed from Helena Ridge.

Castle Mountain Fire Lookout Site

Distance: 3.9 km (2.4 mi) — Bow Valley Parkway to site of former fire lookout on west aspect of Castle Mountain
Day hike: 1.5—2 hours one way
Elevation gain: 525 m (1720 ft)
Maximum elevation: 1975 m (6480 ft)
Maps: Gem Trek 1:100,000 Banff & Mt. Assiniboine and NTS 1:50,000 Castle Mountain 82-O/5
Trailhead: Parking area at end of short spur road on north side of Bow Valley Parkway, 4.9 km (3.0 mi) north of Castle Junction and 9.0 km (5.6 mi) south of Baker Creek.

0.0 — Trailhead kiosk (elevation 1450 m). Climb steadily through forest.
1.5 — Remnants of an old cabin.
2.2 — Trails narrows and begins ascent across meadows, then switchbacks through small rockbands.
3.9 — Site of former fire lookout (1975 m).

This hike leads to the former site of a fire lookout, one of a network in Banff National Park that was in active service until the 1970s. (For more background, see the author's *Fire Lookout Hikes in the Canadian Rockies*, Luminous Compositions, 1998.)

The open slopes near trail's end offer a bright floral display. The clifftop location grants expansive views west over the Bow Valley into British Columbia, beyond Mt. Temple near Lake Louise to the north, and south to the Sundance Range (with Mt. Assiniboine on the horizon).

Mountain goats might be seen here; the pronounced shelf above on the west face of Castle Mountain is known as Goat Ledge. There is a tiny shelter on Goat Ledge: contact the Alpine Club of Canada (see p. 14) for reservations and information on the approach. This outing is best left for rockclimbers doing technical routes on the buttresses.

The author at site of Castle Mountain Fire Lookout, and north including Mt. Temple on right.

Noseeum Creek

Distance: 3. 3 km (2.0 mi) — Icefields Parkway to "Noseeum Lake"
Off-trail scramble: 1.5—2 hours one way
Elevation gain: 640 m (2100 ft)
Maximum elevation: 2465 m (8085 ft)
Maps: Gem Trek 1:70,000 Bow Lake and Saskatchewan Crossing, and NTS 1:50,000 Hector Lake 82 N/9
Trailhead: Small unmarked parking area on the east side of the Icefields Parkway, 23.0 km (14.3 mi) north of the Trans-Canada Highway and 1.0 km (0.6 mi) south of Mosquito Creek.

0.0 — Unmarked parking area (elevation 1825 m). Head up drainage.

2.0 — End of cirque; to continue, scramble steeply up headwall beside waterfall. At top, head north into basin.

3.3 — "Noseeum Lake" (2465 m).

The derivation of the name of Noseeum Creek is similar to that of nearby Mosquito Creek, although it could just as well have originated because the creek is easy to miss, or because it is unlikely that anyone else will be seen along its course.

Upstream travel is by means of faint trails along the banks or by rockhopping over the jumbled outwash boulders in the creek bed. Soon enter the portals of a narrow valley surrounded by soaring cliffs, jagged pinnacles, and massive rockslides.

The headwall reached after 2 km of relatively level travel can be ascended by scrambling steeply up either left or right of a high waterfall, depending on whether one's preference is for being among trees or on more open rocky slopes. The cascade at the start of this tricky climb drops over the lowermost of a series of bands of grey limestone below the high tarn that is the creek's source.

It is therefore unofficially referred to as "Noseeum Lake." Mountain goats may be observed in this remote alpine setting. The lake can be circumnavigated with a little manoeuvering over the small cliffs on the east shore.

Making the circuit of "Noseeum Lake" gives views west to ice-clad Mt. Balfour, and—nearer at hand—to the white blanket of the Molar Glacier less then 2 km to the south. This permanent accumulation of ice covers the northeastern aspect of the peak known as "Andromache" after the wife of the mythological Hector in the Greek classics. The connection with neighbouring Mt. Hector is tenuous since that prominent peak was named in honour of Sir James Hector, a decidedly more contemporary and less evanescent figure.

Mosquito Creek

Distance: 6.4 km (4.0 mi) — Icefields Parkway to Mosquito Creek backcountry campground
Day hike/backpack: 1.5—2 hours one way
Elevation gain: 145 m (475 ft)
Maximum elevation: 1975 m (6480 ft)
Maps: Gem Trek 1:70,000 Bow Lake and Saskatchewan Crossing, and NTS 1:50,000 Hector Lake 82 N/9
Trailhead: Parking area on west side of Icefields Parkway, south of Mosquito Creek bridge [serves for youth hostel as well], 24.0 km (14.9 mi) north of the Trans-Canada Highway and 9.0 km (5.6 mi) south of the Crowfoot Glacier viewpoint.

0.0 — Trailhead kiosk (elevation 1830 m) on east side of highway north of bridge (opposite the campground entrance). Climb steeply initially, then more gradually.
5.3 — Cross footbridge (1935 m) over northwest tributary of Mosquito Creek.
6.4 — Backcountry campground (1975 m).

Despite the inauspicious name, the Mosquito Creek area deserves to be visited. Because of its elevation, this area can actually offer respite from biting insects when they are at their peak lower down.

The trail rises gently except near the beginning. Once on the flats of the creek, there are views ahead, and back to the steep east face of Bow Peak. The easily reached backcountry campground can serve as a base for day hikes on the *Molar Pass* and *North Molar Pass/Fish Lakes* trails.

Gnawed patches of bark on the conifers near the end of this trail confirm the preference of porcupines for subalpine habitat.

Adventurous cross-country travellers can branch off at km 5.3 to explore the valley of the north tributary of Mosquito Creek. There is a faint path along the west bank at first, but it soon disappears. However, the terrain is open enough to permit relatively straightforward travel through the lush subalpine meadows and forest.

View from Mosquito Creek backcountry campground.

169

North Molar Pass/Fish Lakes

Distance: 11.4 km (7.1 mi) — Mosquito Creek backcountry campground to Pipestone River via North Molar Pass
Day hike/backpack: 3—3.5 hours one way
Elevation gain: 620 m (2035 ft)
Elevation loss: 615 m (2015 ft)
Maximum elevation: 2590 m (8495 ft)
Maps: Gem Trek 1:70,000 Bow Lake and Saskatchewan Crossing, and NTS 1:50,000 Hector Lake 82 N/9
Trailhead: End of *Mosquito Creek* trail at km 6.4 (see p. 169).

0.0 — Mosquito Creek backcountry campground (elevation 1975 m). Cross footbridge to south side of creek.

0.5 — Cross footbridge to north side of Mosquito Creek.

1.0 — Keep straight (2070 m); *Molar Pass* trail to right. Climb steadily, reaching alpine meadows in 500 metres.

2.4 — Travel north of "Mosquito Lake."

4.1 — Begin steep climb.

5.1 — North Molar Pass (2590 m). Descend to south.

8.4 — Backcountry campground midway along north shore of Upper Fish Lake.

9.0 — Warden cabin down to left.

9.3 — Keep left at junction north of Lower Fish Lake; right leads to outfitter's camping area.

9.7 — Cross outlet stream from Lower Fish Lake and begin steep descent.

11.2 — Two fords in quick succession: of outlet from Fish Lakes and of Pipestone RIver (1975 m).

11.4 — *Upper Pipestone Valley* trail (1980 m) at km 9.9.

Summit of Molar Mountain to south beyond North Molar Pass.

Upper Fish Lake.

The most frequent extension to the *Mosquito Creek* trail is that over North Molar Pass to Upper Fish Lake. The route, which becomes muddy when wet, leads up through extensive meadows to a height of almost 2600 m. (This is the second highest maintained trail in Banff National Park, after Sentinel Pass near Moraine Lake—for which see *Hiking Lake Louise*.)

Descending from North Molar Pass, lose some 350 metres of elevation en route to the backcountry campground midway along the north shore of Upper Fish Lake. Along the way there are views east over the deep valley of the Pipestone River to a range of which the most striking mountain is Cataract Peak, rising to over 3300 m.

The importance of carrying a topographic map was emphasized for the author on a trip in 1988 when he met a European couple at the Mosquito Creek campground who had gone up to North Molar Pass intending to continue to Upper Fish Lake, but who (without a proper map) had turned back because they expected to see the lake below. They were also uncertain about where to head since snow covered the trail, which is common at that elevation until well into summer. For safety and peace of mind, take along a detailed map!

The trail east of Upper Fish Lake runs near Lower Fish Lake before heading steeply down to the Pipestone River. If backpacking over Pipestone Pass, distance and elevation gain can be reduced by taking a traverse via a bench above the valley. The trail, which starts at a ford of the creek north of the Fish Lakes warden cabin, is faint in places. Once on the narrow path it stays high all the way to the pass, travelling by the small body of water known as "Moose Lake" (grid reference 553237). Near the end, keep to the prominent ridgecrest between two drainages, then cut across the bare shale slope to the *Upper Pipestone Valley* trail.

An off-trail variation of the *North Molar Pass/Fish Lakes* trail is to scramble along the ridges southwest of the pass, crowned with a prominent wedge-shaped peak. A highlight of this outing is a seldom seen view from the east of the abrupt towers of Dolomite Peak. (For more information, see the author's *Ridgewalks in the Canadian Rockies*, Luminous Compositions, 2001.)

Molar Pass

Distance: 17.3 km (10.7 mi) — *North Molar Pass/Fish Lakes* trail to Pipestone RIver via Molar Creek
Day hike/backpack: 4.5—5 hours one way
Elevation gain: 290 m (950 ft)
Elevation loss: 550 m (1805 ft)
Maximum elevation: 2360 m (7740 ft)
Maps: Gem Trek 1:70,000 Bow Lake and Saskatchewan Crossing, and NTS 1:50,000 Hector Lake 82 N/9
Trailhead: Km 1.0 of *North Molar Pass/Fish Lakes* trail (see p. 171).

0.0 — Sign (elevation 2070 m). Veer right and cross stream; straight leads to North Molar Pass and Fish Lakes. Climb steadily.

2.5 — Begin steep climb traversing across scree slope below headwall.

2.9 — Molar Pass (2360 m). Trail continues south through meadows.

3.3 — Turn right at faint junction and descend; straight fades out.

5.8 — Begin steep descent through forest toward Molar Creek.

7.3 — Cross creek, usually by rockhopping. Ambiguous sections of trail in valley bottom.

13.1 — Backcountry campground at grid reference 555154.

15.7 — Trail turns away from creek to climb over forested ridge.

17.3 — Junction (1810 m) with *Upper Pipestone Valley* trail on west bank of Pipestone River. On opposite side of river, *Lower Pipestone Valley* trail turns right and trail toward Skoki Valley goes straight (see *Hiking Lake Louise*).

The route to Molar Pass branches right off the *North Molar Pass/Fish Lakes* trail and winds steadily up through meadows. To breach the headwall below the pass, the trail takes an indirect approach that slopes up from the east.

The saddle grants a panoramic view past sheer cliffs over the valley of Mosquito Creek. To the south loom the dark rocky towers of Molar Mountain, after which the creek and the pass are named. The 3022 m summit was first reached in 1901 by surveyor/mountaineer J.J. McArthur and the indomitable Tom Wilson.

This spot is not the best for an appreciation of the similarity of the mountain's shape to the double-crowned type of tooth, but the peak looks impressive nonetheless. Also in sight is the glaciated north side of Mt. Hector. In the distance across the Pipestone River, over 15 km away, the serrated ranges near Skoki Valley etch their rugged profile on the horizon.

It is rewarding to simply relax or amble about the alpine meadows here. If intent on descending to the Pipestone River, veer right at the faint junction several hundred metres south of the pass and drop toward the valley of Molar Creek.

The going can be vague at first, and again when reach the gravel flats after a steep stint through forest. Keep in mind that the designated backcountry campground can be difficult to locate.

Upper Pipestone Valley

Distance: 18.1 km (11.2 mi) — Molar Creek junction to Pipestone River headwaters
Backpack: 5—6 hours one way
Elevation gain: 630 m (2065 ft)
Maximum elevation: 2440 m (8005 ft)
Maps: Gem Trek 1:70,000 Bow Lake and Saskatchewan Crossing, and NTS 1:50,000 Hector Lake 82 N/9
Trailhead: End of *Molar Pass* trail at km 17.3. (Access to this point can also be gained via the *Lower Pipestone Valley* trail or via Skoki Valley; see the author's *Hiking Lake Louise* guidebook.)

0.0 — Sign (elevation 1810 m). Head north up valley on gradual ascent.
8.9 — Campsite and ford to east side of Pipestone River.
9.9 — Keep straight (1980 m); *North Molar Pass/Fish Lakes* trail to left. Climb steadily.
18.1 — High point (2440 m) in gap northeast of true Pipestone Pass. *Siffleur River* trail continues northwest down valley.

This portion of trail in the Pipestone Valley is markedly better than the lower section (see *Hiking Lake Louise*). It passes through vast meadows with generous views and delivers to the alpine surroundings of Pipestone Pass. The name of the river derives from the shale on its banks, which was used by Native people to fashion pipe bowls and other artifacts.

The eccentric Earl of Southesk, who hauled along volumes of Shakespeare on what was a glorified hunting safari, crossed Pipestone Pass in 1859. He gave a description of "crossing miles of bleak open moor, with not a tree in sight, and only enough of the surrounding rocks and mountains visible through the mist to show how much noble scenery was being lost."

Highlights of this trail include views of Cataract Peak—elevation 3333 m (10,932 ft)—with a hanging glacier on its shoulder, and of twin icefalls descending from the Drummond Glacier to the southeast.

Note that the end of this trail is a gap northeast of and slightly higher than the actual Pipestone Pass.

Pipestone River in meadows section of *Upper Pipestone Valley* trail.

Helen Creek

Distance: 4.9 km (3.0 mi) — Icefields Parkway to Helen Lake
Day hike/backpack: 1.5—2 hours one way
Elevation gain: 490 m (1605 ft)
Elevation loss: 10 m (33 ft)
Maximum elevation: 2370 m (7775 ft)
Maps: Gem Trek 1:70,000 Bow Lake and Saskatchewan Crossing, and NTS 1:50,000 Hector Lake 82 N/9
Trailhead: Small unmarked parking area on north side of Icefields Parkway west of bridge over Helen Creek, 4.5 km (2.8 mi) north of Mosquito Creek and 4.0 km (2.5 mi) south of Crowfoot Glacier viewpoint.

0.0 — North side of parking area (elevation 1890 m). Climb through forest on narrow path.
0.9 — Descend from terrace (1995 m) toward creek.
1.0 — Cross to north side of Helen Creek (1985 m) and work up valley.
3.0 — Begin steep ascent, forested at first, then breaking into meadows.
3.8 — Trail levels out. Faint path heads northwest toward Helen Lake, contouring to south of knoll east of lake. (Direct off-trail route to Dolomite Pass veers east to climb over ridge before descending north to Katherine Lake.)
4.9 — South end of Helen Lake (2370 m).

This trail up Helen Creek is an alternative to the approach to Helen Lake from the well-marked trailhead opposite the Crowfoot Glacier viewpoint (see next page). Although it begins at a slightly lower elevation, this way is more direct.

The first kilometre is moderately steep; thereafter the trail runs fairly level for 2 km, with views of rugged Dolomite Peak. Then climb up a slope of subalpine forest to break into the open within 1 km of Helen Lake. The path becomes vague after topping out above the trees, but the lake is easy to find on the far side of the knoll ahead.

Grizzly bears frequent this area; there are numerous examples of their diggings for roots and bulbs.

If headed for Dolomite Pass, save time and elevation gain by doubling back cross-country through cliffbands southwest of Katherine Lake. Then descend to the *Dolomite Pass and Creek* trail at the north end of that body of water.

Helen Lake

Distance: 6.0 km (3.7 mi) — Icefields Parkway to Helen Lake
Day hike/backpack: 2—2.5 hours one way
Elevation gain: 420 m (1380 ft)
Maximum elevation: 2370 m (7775 ft)
Maps: Gem Trek 1:70,000 Bow Lake and Saskatchewan Crossing, and NTS 1:50,000 Hector Lake 82 N/9
Trailhead: Parking area on short spur north off Icefields Parkway opposite the Crowfoot Glacier viewpoint, 9.5 km (5.9 mi) north of Mosquito Creek and 2.5 km (1.6 mi) south of the Num-Ti-Jah Lodge turnoff.

0.0 — Trailhead kiosk (elevation 1950 m). Climb steeply at first, then more gradually as travel east.
2.5 — Break into meadows and ascend steeply.
3.5 — Head northwest after crossing ridge; almost level going.
5.0 — Cross Helen Creek in small gorge.
6.0 — South end of Helen Lake (2370 m).

 This highline route leads to one of the more easily accessible alpine areas in Banff National Park. The wildflower displays along this outing are excellent. Another notable presence—though not welcome at close quarters, so be alert—is that of grizzly bears, which are particularly fond of the corms (bulbs) of the glacier lilies that grow here in abundance.

 Helen Lake and nearby Katherine Lake are named for two of the daughters of H.P. Nichols, a New York clergyman who later became president of the American Alpine Club. The Rev. Nichols made several mountaineering trips to the Canadian Rockies; he was a member of a party that crossed Dolomite Pass and came upon these lakes in 1898. (A third daughter, Margaret, had her name given to a lake near Hector Lake; see p. 113.)

Crowfoot Glacier and Bow Lake from *Helen Lake* trail.

Dolomite Pass and Creek

Distance: 19.6 km (12.2 mi) — Helen Lake to confluence of Dolomite Creek and Siffleur River
Backpack: 6—7 hours one way
Elevation gain: 155 m (510 ft)
Elevation loss: 725 m (2380 ft)
Maximum elevation: 2500 m (8200 ft)
Maps: Gem Trek 1:70,000 Bow Lake and Saskatchewan Crossing, and NTS 1:50,000 Hector Lake 82 N/9 and Siffleur River 82 N/16
Trailhead: South end of Helen Lake, reached via either *Helen Creek* trail (see p. 174) or *Helen Lake* trail (see p. 175).

0.0 — South end of Helen Lake (elevation 2370 m). Travel above east shore of lake and climb steeply through cliffband.

0.9 — High point (2500 m) on wide saddle at base of south ridge of Cirque Peak (see *Cirque Peak* trail, p. 178). Descend steeply to east.

2.1 — North end of Katherine Lake (2370 m); direct route from *Helen Creek* trail joins here, while *Dolomite Peak Circuit* trail leaves from here. Head northeast; trail vague in places.

2.9 — Dolomite Pass (2395 m). Descend north into drainage of Dolomite Creek.

6.4 — Travel west of gorge with waterfall. Descend steeply.

7.1 — Ford Dolomite Creek to east bank: first of three fords in next 1.5 km.

11.0 — Ford Dolomite Creek to west bank.

11.1 — Cross tributary stream. Trail levels out.

12.6 — Keep to west of extensive flats on sometimes sketchy trail.

16.3 — Campsite near southwest corner of Isabella Lake.

16.4 — Warden cabin. Follow west shore of lake.

19.6 — Junction (1800 m) near confluence of Dolomite Creek and Siffleur River. *Siffleur River* trail to east; Banff National Park boundary 1.6 km north. (Rough trail continues north through provincially administered Siffleur Wilderness Area to reach footbridge over North Saskatchewan River approximately 27.5 km from boundary.)

Cow moose and calf.

North down Dolomite Creek from near Dolomite Pass.

Dolomite Peak and its associated pass and creek take their names from a resemblance to the Dolomites of Europe, as noticed by a late-nineteenth century climbing party. Dolomite Pass grants dramatic views of the northern aspect of the peak and outlying ridges.

After climbing to the lofty saddle above Helen Lake, the trail descends to Katherine Lake and makes its way toward the pass over open, rolling, tundra-like terrain with several small lakes. The odds are very good that hoary marmots will be seen in these alpine surroundings.

A side trip from near the head of Dolomite Creek is to Alice Lake, nestled in a high cirque to the east. Not to be forgotten when her daughters had their names bestowed on various lakes (see p. 175), the Rev. H.P. Nichols' wife is remembered in this jewel in a rugged setting.

Keep to the west side of Dolomite Creek as descending its valley, passing a gorge with an impressive waterfall. A number of crossings are required farther downstream, although it may be possible to avoid some by means of trees that have fallen across the stream.

One section of trail veers away from the watercourse to pass around a huge rockslide: it was on this stretch that the author once suddenly came upon a bull moose. Given that it was autumn, with the rut in progress, and that the bull was giving him a baleful stare, he moved on.

The hiking trail does not cross the flats above Isabella Lake (as may be shown on some maps), rather avoiding numerous fords by keeping to the west on a narrow path. The campsite near the southwest shore of Isabella Lake serves as a good overnight stop, especially if fishing is on the agenda. (This is the only place where angling is permitted within the Siffleur and Clearwater drainages.)

The trail follows Dolomite Creek to just above its confluence with the Siffleur River, where the *Siffleur River* trail begins.

177

Cirque Peak

Distance: 1.3 km (0.8 mi) — *Dolomite Pass and Creek* trail to summit of Cirque Peak
Off-trail scramble: 1—1.5 hour(s) one way
Elevation gain: 493 m (1617 ft)
Maximum elevation: 2993 m (9817 ft)
Maps: Gem Trek 1:70,000 Bow Lake and Saskatchewan Crossing, and NTS 1:50,000 Hector Lake 82 N/9
Trailhead: Km 0.9 of *Dolomite Pass and Creek* trail (see p. 176).

0.0 — Wide saddle (elevation 2500 m) at base of south ridge of Cirque Peak. Climb steeply up scree slope to north.
1.3 — Summit of Cirque Peak (2993 m).

The ascent of Cirque Peak is essentially a scree slog, though well-defined cross-bedding and ripple marks in the sedimentary rock can give cause for a pause. Despite the less-than-glamorous route, the effort is worthwhile for the excellent panorama from the top. (There is a little dip to be negotiated to reach the high point.)

First climbed in August, 1899, Cirque Peak—whose elevation is just seven metres shy of 3000 m—reveals a vast spread of the Rockies. Mt. Assiniboine is visible almost 100 km to the south, while glacier-draped Mt. Columbia can be discerned nearly as far to the north. Myriad peaks rise in the interval between the two. Close by is the Crowfoot Glacier, its entire extent visible. The Bow Glacier can be seen flowing almost into the lake that feeds Bow Glacier Falls, and there is a view of the south end of Isabella Lake below braided channels of Dolomite Creek.

There is a surprisingly large icefield on the northeast side of Cirque Peak. A saunter along the north ridge brings Alice Lake into sight to the east and grants a view of the dramatic north face of the mountain.

The descent back to Helen Lake, which can be made via the crest of the cliffs above its west side, returns one to such sights as marsh marigolds at the outlet and robins flitting about.

Summit of Cirque Peak from north ridge.

Dolomite Peak Circuit

Distance: 7.0 km (4.3 mi) — Katherine Lake to *Mosquito Creek* trail
Off-trail scramble: 2—2.5 hours one way
Elevation gain: 175 m (575 ft)
Elevation loss: 630 m (2065 ft)
Maximum elevation: 2545 m (8350 ft)
Maps: Gem Trek 1:70,000 Bow Lake and Saskatchewan Crossing, and NTS 1:50,000 Hector Lake 82 N/9
Trailhead: Km 2.1 of *Dolomite Pass and Creek* trail (see p. 176).

0.0 — North end of Katherine Lake (elevation 2370 m). Head east and then southeast toward the saddle at grid reference 443264.
2.3 — Saddle (2545 m). Descend to southeast.
7.0 — Junction (1915 m) with *Mosquito Creek* trail at approximately km 4.6.

This route is more often used as an advanced cross-country ski trip, yet provides an unusual outing during hiking season.

Climb steadily southeast from the Dolomite Pass area, enjoying the spectacular rocky pinnacles and towers around the head of the cirque on the north side of Dolomite Peak. Aim for the saddle below the steeply sloping grey slabs of an unnamed peak to the east.

From the saddle the view to the south includes the glaciated north side of Mt. Hector. A steady descent leads to a tributary that flows into Mosquito Creek from the west: This can be followed down, or a more direct line made through open forest (as taken on skis to avoid a terrain trap in the V-notch). Some bushwhacking may be required to reach the *Mosquito Creek* trail.

Pika.

Siffleur River

Distance: 19.3 km (12.0 mi) — Dolomite Creek to Siffleur River headwaters
Backpack: 6—7 hours one way
Elevation gain: 660 m (2165 ft)
Elevation loss: 20 m (65 ft)
Maximum elevation: 2440 m (8005 ft)
Maps: Gem Trek 1:70,000 Bow Lake and Saskatchewan Crossing [northern portion of trail], and NTS 1:50,000 Siffleur River 82 N/16 and Hector Lake 82 N/9
Trailhead: End of *Dolomite Pass and Creek* trail at km 19.6 (see p. 172).

0.0 — Sign (elevation 1800 m). Head east.
0.1 — Cross Dolomite Creek to east side (**caution:** difficult ford in high water). Head southeast up valley of Siffleur River, climbing gradually.
3.5 — High point (1925 m). Descend toward river.
4.0 — Ford Siffleur River (1905 m) to east side.
5.8 — Designated camping area at grid reference 441356: camp must be made within 100 metres of the sign.
9.0 — Pass above abandoned warden cabin. Moderate climb to vast meadows at head of valley.
16.3 — Keep straight (2255 m); *Clearwater Valley* trail to left.
19.3 — High point (2440 m) in gap northeast of true Pipestone Pass. *Upper Pipestone Valley* trail descends to southeast; direct option to Upper Fish Lake to right (see p. 171).

It is possible to go down the Siffleur Valley from the end of the *Dolomite Pass and Creek* trail all the way to the North Saskatchewan River in about 29 km, but it's a rather masochistic trudge along old seismic lines and through forest regenerating after a 1974 fire. Plus there are potentially hazardous fords.

Most backpackers head upstream on this trail. Note that this also entails a couple of fords, the first of which—across Dolomite Creek—should be approached with caution. The ford of the Siffleur River at km 4.0 is usually easy. Less than 2 km farther upstream is the designated camping site in this Special Preservation zone. The ruins of a log cabin are nearby.

The trail ascends steadily up the valley, which is interspersed with forested sections and large meadows. Pass a bit of history in the form of an abandoned warden cabin at km 9.0. The upper reaches of the Siffleur River are in wide-open country: magnificent in fine weather but most uncomfortable when inclement conditions prevail.

It is precisely this sort of country, nevertheless, that attracts and supports a small group of caribou. An albino individual has been reported, which is an indication of the "precarious situation with regard to [...] limited genetic diversity" (*Special Resources of Banff National Park*, Warden Service, 1986) that these animals face.

The caribou of the Siffleur River area are the rarest ungulates in Banff National Park; they represent the southernmost distribution of the species in Alberta. Caribou are the only members of the deer family (which includes moose, elk, and the

Abandoned Siffleur River warden cabin.

various species of deer) in which both sexes sport antlers—albeit smaller on the females than the males.

After passing the junction with the start of the *Clearwater Valley* trail, this trail traverses the lower western slopes of Devon Mountain to reach the end of the *Upper Pipestone Valley* trail. Note that the route does not go through the true Pipestone Pass but a slightly higher gap some 900 metres to the northeast.

Clearwater Valley

Distance: 29.2 km (18.1 mi) — Siffleur RIver to Banff National Park boundary in Clearwater Valley
Backpack: 1.5—2 days one way
Elevation gain: 80 m (260 ft)
Elevation loss: 570 m (1870 ft)
Maximum elevation: 2335 m (7660 ft)
Maps: NTS 1:50,000 Hector Lake 82 N/9, Siffleur River 82 N/16, and Forbidden Creek 82-O/13
Trailhead: Km 16.3 of *Siffleur River* trail (see p. 180).

0.0 — Sign (elevation 2255 m). Head east up into open rolling terrain.

1.1 — Clearwater Pass (2335 m). Continue northeast over undulating meadows, descending slightly.

2.7 — Travel north of Upper Devon Lake and begin steep descent east toward Clearwater River.

9.6 — Reach meadows along river; travel northeast.

12.0 — Warden cabin.

13.3 — Travel along northwest shore of Clearwater Lake.

17.0 — Cross Martin Creek to north side (if ford is not feasible at this point, head upstream to wade across at outlet of Martin Lake).

17.2 — Pass waterfall in small gorge on Martin Creek.

17.8 — Travel along north shore of Trident Lake. Campsites near east end of lake.

23.2 — Enter large meadow.

24.1 — Ford Malloch Creek.

27.4 — Keep straight (1795 m); *Indianhead Creek* trail to left.

28.1 — Ford Indianhead Creek.

28.2 — Warden cabin; trail continues east.

29.2 — Banff National Park boundary (1765 m). To connect with *Peters Creek/ Divide Creek* trail, continue east some 2.5 km and ford Clearwater River to south bank (the point to cross to may be marked by a moose antler on tree).

The Clearwater is the most remote valley in Banff National Park accessible by trail. The valley's significance, particularly as wildlife habitat, is indicated by its designation as part of the Clearwater—Siffleur Special Preservation zone. (Unlike in the Siffleur, random camping is permitted in this valley. Fishing is not.)

An indication of the wild nature of the Clearwater Valley is the presence of wolverines: these carnivores require large ranges—males may use up to 2000 square kilometres. This valley is also the territory of a wolf pack.

This trail receives far more visitation by horseback parties than by travellers on foot, but experienced backpackers can gain an intimate appreciation of this back-of-beyond corner of the Canadian Rockies. Starting off the *Siffleur River* trail, climb a short distance to the undulating hillocks of Clearwater Pass, then descend slightly to Upper Devon Lake.

The Devon Lakes host one of only two colonies of cliff swallows in the alpine

Northeast from Malloch Creek meadows on *Clearwater Valley* trail.

zone of Banff National Park (the other is at Redoubt Lake near Lake Louise).

Clearwater Pass is the northern limit for subalpine larch in Alberta; even though large areas of seemingly suitable upper subalpine habitat occur further north, the trees do not grow there. North of the pass rise the steep, rocky tiers of Mt. Willingdon, at 3373 m (11,063 ft) the highest peak for some distance around.

The trail drops steeply from Clearwater Pass through forest to the more level valley bottom, the river now augmented by a number of tributaries. The age of the warden cabin by the flats above Clearwater Lake is indicated by the graffiti dating from the 1930s that is carved into its logs.

Elk congregate in the marshy shallows around Trident Lake, possibly acting like moose as they stand in belly-deep water and duck their heads for aquatic vegetation. The cascading of the waterfall on Roaring Creek can, despite the raucous-sounding name, act as a lullaby if stay overnight here.

The vast meadows around the confluence of Malloch Creek with the Clearwater allow improved views of the surroundings, including Mt. Harris to the west and Mt. Peters to the east (both named for topographical surveyors). The junction with the *Indianhead Creek* trail is 700 metres before the ford of that creek. Below the crossing, just downstream from the meeting of the creek with the Clearwater, are spectacular hoodoos (earth pillars) on the south bank of the river.

The trail continues down the valley beyond the Banff National Park boundary; to reach the Red Deer River, go approximately 1 km to a faint path branching right off the main trail just after a large meadow and an outfitter's camp. This leads in another 1.5 km or so to the crossing of the Clearwater (tricky in high water) to its south bank and the *Peters Creek/Divide Creek* trail.

Indianhead Creek

Distance: 13.0 km (8.1 mi) — Clearwater Valley to Indianhead Creek headwaters
Day/hike/backpack: 3.5—4 hours one way
Elevation gain: 635 m (2085 ft)
Elevation loss: 155 m (510 ft)
Maximum elevation: 2275 m (7460 ft)
Map: NTS 1:50,000 Siiffleur River 82 N/16
Trailhead: Km 27.4 of *Clearwater Valley* trail (see p. 182).

0.0 — Sign (elevation 1795 m). Climb steadily to west.
3.4 — Skirt large meadow and begin steep climb to north.
4.7 — Saddle; veer northwest and keep climbing.
5.3 — High point (2190 m) just west of small knoll. Descend north into bowl.
5.6 — Low point (2140 m) in bowl. Climb to north.
7.0 — High point (2180 m). Descend steeply toward Indianhead Creek.
8.0 — Trail levels out (2075 m) above west bank.
11.0 — Cross to east side of creek.
13.0 — Saddle (2275 m) at headwaters of Indianhead Creek, and Banff National Park boundary. Rough trail descends north to Ram River and ultimately, in approx. 37 km, to footbridge over North Saskatchewan River at Kootenay Plains.

This is a rewarding side trip when backpacking in the Clearwater Valley. The trail at first runs almost parallel to the trail along the Clearwater River, rising only gradually. Then, after a meadow, it climbs steeply to a saddle.

Pikas will probably be heard, and may be seen, in the rockslide below the saddle. Beyond, drop to Indianhead Creek, whose lower stretch is a deep gorge not readily negotiated. The terrain from this point on is more open, with continuous views of the nearby summits, including Wampum Peak—elevation 2864 m (9394 ft)—first ascended in 1919 by members of the Topographical Survey.

The trail continues to the saddle at the headwaters of Indianhead Creek, which is also the park boundary. This has confusingly been referred to as Whiterabbit Pass, which seems inappropriate since Whiterabbit Creek is at least 10 km distant.

Indianhead Creek is one of only three known locations in Banff National Park for spider plant—not the common household one, but a rare alpine wildflower (*Saxifraga flagellaris*) that here is near the southern limit of its circumpolar range. Its common name comes from whip-like runners radiating from its rosette of basal leaves; each of the runners ends in a tiny, strawberry-like offset that establishes its own roots.

Peters Creek/Divide Creek

Distance: 25.4 km (15.7 mi) — Clearwater River to Red Deer River
Backpack: 1.5—2 days one way
Elevation gain: 910 m (2985 ft)
Elevation loss: 865 m (2835 ft)
Maximum elevation: 2395 m (7855 ft)
Maps: NTS 1:50,000 Forbidden Creek 82-O/13 and Barrier Mountain 82-O/12
Trailhead: Point on south bank of Clearwater River, approx. 2.5 km east of end of *Clearwater Valley* trail at Banff National Park boundary (see p. 182).

0.0 — Point on south bank of Clearwater River (elevation 1725 m), possibly marked by moose antler on tree. Head south.

0.3 — Cross stream below low terrace.

0.4 — Campsite. Keep south through meadows.

0.9 — Veer right at sign with hiker symbol; straight ahead is horse trail up gorge of Peters Creek. Trail vague.

1.4 — Enter forest at tall blazed tree in southeast corner of meadow. Begin steady climb.

3.0 — High point (1920 m). Descend toward creek, gradually at first, then more steeply. (cont. p. 186)

North from saddle between Peters Creek and Divide Creek; Mt. Peters on right.

(cont. from p. 185)
4.6 — Turn right to head upstream where rejoin horse trail (1860 m).

6.2 — Ford Peters Creek to east bank: first of three crossings in 400 metres.

12.4 — Cross to west side of Peters Creek southwest of "Shale Pass." Climb steeply.

13.8 — Saddle (2395 m) between Peters Creek and Divide Creek. Descend south into drainage of Divide Creek.

15.2 — Start (2290 m) short climb to terrace.

15.3 — Resume (2315 m) descent down valley.

17.1 — Warden cabin. Keep south; do not head southeast down gorge of Divide Creek.

17.4 — Cross Divide Creek (2115 m) and begin ascent over shoulder to south.

18.8 — High point (2270 m) on shoulder. Steady descent southeast.

25.4 — Junction (1770 m) with *Red Deer River* trail at km 1.8.

The north end of this trail begins on the south bank of the Clearwater River some 2.5 km east of the Banff National Park boundary. It first leads to an old campsite at the north end of a large meadow, then passes through a narrow band of trees into a larger meadow. Here veer right at a sign with hiker symbol.

Going this way avoids several fords on the horse trail through the canyon. The route is vague through the meadow, but well-defined from the point where it enters the forest at a tall, blazed tree. Climb steadily over a ridge of Mt. Peters, then drop into the drainage of Peters Creek to join the horse trail (this intersection could easily be missed if coming from the south).

There are three fords in quick succession, then keep east of the creek as working steadily up toward its headwaters. A final ford just as reach treeline precedes the last kilometre and a bit to the pass. (A short side trip could be made up switchbacks to the gap on the park boundary known as Shale Pass at grid reference 736353, on the other side of which lies a tributary of Forbidden Creek.)

In the saddle between Peters Creek and Divide Creek can be found felled poles with wooden insulators still attached: these held the telephone line that once connected the network of warden cabins, before the advent of radio.

As descending toward Divide Creek, there is the chance—especially if it is during fall migration—that a large raptor such as a northern harrier may be gliding over the open slopes in search of rodent prey.

A waterhole several hundred metres west of the Divide Creek warden cabin is an excellent place to observe wildlife, particularly in early morning and late evening.

The trail continues south over a shoulder (not down the drainage) and steadily downhill through forest to intersect the *Red Deer River* trail.

Red Deer River

Distance: 26.7 km (16.6 mi) — *Upper Cascade Valley* trail to Red Deer Lakes
Backpack: 1.5—2 days one way
Elevation gain: 345 m (1130 ft)
Maximum elevation: 2095 m (6870 ft)
Maps: NTS 1:50,000 Barrier Mountain 82-O/12 and Hector Lake 82 N/9
Trailhead: Km 10.9 of *Upper Cascade Valley* trail (see p. 189).

0.0 — Sign (elevation 1750 m). Head west off former fire road.
1.4 — Ford Divide Creek to west bank.
1.8 — Keep straight (1770 m); *Peters Creek/Divide Creek* trail to right.
6.1 — Ford McConnell Creek to west bank.
7.3 — Start of 2-km-long gorge with waterfalls.
11.5 — Keep straight; Horseshoe Lake (may be shown as Skeleton Lake on some maps) 1.0 km to left via ford of Red Deer River.
13.0 — Cross tributary (possibly via fallen trees).
13.5 — Keep straight; warden cabin 100 metres to left.
20.0 — Keep straight; Douglas Lake 3.0 km to left via ford of Red Deer River.
21.8 — Ford Drummond Creek to west bank. Begin steady climb.
24.5 — Keep straight; Natural Bridge 2.5 km to left via ford of Red Deer River.
26.3 — Pass warden cabin.
26.7 — Junction (2095 m) at Red Deer Lakes. Options from here include the *Pipestone River from Red Deer Lakes* and *Red Deer Lakes from Baker Lake* trails (see *Hiking Lake Louise*).

Leaving the *Upper Cascade Valley* trail near the high bridge over the Red Deer River, this trail follows the river to its source at the Red Deer Lakes. The name of the river is a translation of the Cree *was-ka-soo*, which means "many elk." (The several subspecies of wapiti or American elk are the New World forms of the smaller European red deer.) The abundant elk in this valley support a wolf pack.

Wildlife, particularly elk and bighorn sheep, frequent the natural mineral licks along this stretch of the Red Deer River, the heaviest use taking place in (cont. p. 188)

Mountain goat at mineral lick.

(cont. from p. 187) May and June. The elements present, which include calcium, sulphur, magnesium, sodium, potassium, and phosphorus, supplement what is obtained in forage. These additional intakes are important for metabolic processes such as hair and bone growth, pregnancy, and lactation.

The side trips off this trail to Horseshoe Lake, Douglas Lake, and the Natural Bridge all require fords of the Red Deer River, always to be respected and best left until at least late summer.

Moose may be sighted in the marshy area that the trail passes after the junction at km 13.5.

Two pioneering botanists are honoured in names along the way: David Douglas (1798-1834), who identified the Douglas-fir, and Thomas Drummond, who first collected the widespread yellow mountain avens (whose scientific name is *Dryas drummondii*). It is fitting that the landscape features named after these two stalwarts are in close proximity, especially given that their paths crossed in western Canada in June, 1827. Being Scots, they did not miss the opportunity to go collecting together even though they were professional rivals.

Mt. Douglas towers above the west shore of Douglas Lake; in the distance to the south glimmers the extensive Bonnet Glacier—above which rise numerous mountains, including South Bonnet Peak (see p. 161). A rough trail, which eventually disappears altogether, leads along the west shore of Douglas Lake toward the Valley of the Hidden Lakes...for most, they remain so because of their remoteness.

The crossing of Drummond Creek requires care. The sudden gap of the creek gives a glimpse of the vast Drummond Glacier, which is surrounded by Mt. Drummond and its outliers. Particularly eye-catching from Drummond Creek are the high, vertical northeastern cliffs of Pipestone Mountain.

The trail rises steadily to come into view of Skoki and Fossil mountains before reaching the Red Deer Lakes, which represent the western end of this trail. (For options beyond, see *Hiking Lake Louise*.)

North from summit of South Bonnet Peak, including Douglas Lake right of centre.

188

Upper Cascade Valley

Distance: 55.5 km (34.4 mi) — Red Deer River Valley to north end of *Lower Cascade Valley* trail

Backpack: 2.5—3 days one way
Elevation gain: 830 m (2720 ft)
Elevation loss: 850 m (2790 ft)
Maximum elevation: 2260 m (7415 ft)
Maps: Gem Trek 1:100,000 Banff & Mt. Assiniboine [southern portion of trail] and NTS 1:50,000 Barrier Mountain 82-O/12 and Castle Mountain 82-O/5
Trailhead: Banff National Park boundary in valley of the Red Deer River, approximately 11 km west via old road from Scalp Creek (its two channels must be forded on foot, bridge removed) 2 km south of the buildings of park-operated Ya-Ha-Tinda Ranch. To get to the trailhead, turn north off Highway 1A west of Cochrane and east of Morley onto the Forestry Trunk Road (Highway 940). Take this (gravel most of the way, winding and narrow) to the bridge over the Red Deer River. Turn left immediately after the bridge and drive about 23 km to the entrance to Ya-Ha-Tinda Ranch, then 3 km farther to the parking area at Scalp Creek on a short spur south of the locked gate before the ranch buildings.

0.0 — Gate (elevation 1660 m) at park boundary. Head west on old road.

6.4 — Unmarked junction (1705 m) with *Tyrrell Creek* and *Elkhorn Summit* trails. Ford Tyrrell Creek to west bank. Pass through large meadow, then climb gradually.

9.5 — High point (1800 m). Descend to west.

10.9 — Keep straight (1750 m); *Red Deer River* trail to right.

11.1 — Cross bridge high above gorge of Red Deer RIver.

11.8 — Keep straight; warden cabin to right. Begin steady climb.

19.8 — Sign for route to Snowflake Lake (1.5 km to southwest).

20.0 — Snow Creek Summit (2260 m). Descend gradually to southeast down valley of Snow Creek.

22.5 — Grouse Lake 1 km to northeast.

26.5 — Harrison Lake 3.8 km to west.

29.9 — Ford Panther River (1875 m) to south bank (hazardous in high water).

30.0 — Keep straight; *Upper Panther River* trail to west.

30.2 — Ford Wigmore Creek to east bank and warden cabin. Keep straight; *Lower Panther River* trail to east. Continue south, climbing up valley of Wigmore Creek.

32.5 — First of two fords of Wigmore Creek in 300 metres.

35.5 — Cross outlet at north end of Wigmore Lake.

37.6 — Wigmore Summit (2005 m). Descend steadily down valley of Cuthead Creek.

40.4 — Horse trails west to Cuthead Lake (4.5 km) and east to Bighorn Lake [may be unnamed on some maps] (5 km).

40.5 — Ford Cuthead Creek.

41.5 — Ford Cuthead Creek.

42.3 — Beaver dam may be built partially on old road.

42.4 — Cross Cuthead Creek, possibly via culvert. (cont. p. 190)

(Cont. from p. 189)
42.5 — Keep straight; shortcut toward Flints Park to right.
43.2 — Site of former "Cuthead College" warden training centre.
44.6 — Cross Cuthead Creek.
46.4 — Keep straight (1735 m); *Flints Park* trail to right.
50.8 — Pass by high stockades on left used in past to capture elk (1675 m).
53.0 — High point (1725 m).
55.5 — Connection (1640 m) with north end of *Lower Cascade Valley* trail. Back-country campground and *Dormer Pass and River* trail to east.

This long trail along an abandoned fire road allows mostly easy access into the remote front ranges of northeastern Banff National Park. The main qualifiers of the otherwise straightforward travel on this route are the presence of grizzly bears throughout and the requirement for a series of fords, that of the Panther River being of most concern.

It was formerly possible to drive to the east boundary of the park in the Red Deer River Valley from the Ya-Ha-Tinda Ranch; now that the bridges over Scalp Creek are gone, there is a trek of 11 km along the old road to get to the trailhead.

The first ford on this trail is at Tyrrell Creek, where two unmarked side trails branch off: one north up the creek, the other south across the Red Deer River to Elkhorn Summit. Mts. Tyrrell and White, on either side of the valley ahead, are named for the chief field assistants to geologist/surveyor George Dawson on his 1883 and 1884 expeditions, respectively.

Elk can hardly be missed in the meadows west of Tyrrell Creek; mule deer and moose might also be sighted. The trail climbs slightly, then descends to a bridge over a deep gorge, 200 metres north of which the *Red Deer River* trail heads west.

Beyond the bridge, pass the junction for the Scotch Creek warden cabin, then

The author's random camp near Tyrrell Creek off *Upper Cascade Valley* trail; Bare Range in distance.

start a stiff climb along the lower west slopes of Mt. White toward Snow Creek Summit. It is well worthwhile to venture cross-country the 1.5 km to Snowflake Lake, situated in a large cirque on the east side of the Vermilion Range. On the author's first visit here, he surprised a robin in the alpine meadows near the lake, far from the manicured lawns where the species is often seen. The bird was nesting in a stand of kruppelholz: a German word, meaning "crippled wood," applied to evergreens near treelimit that are stunted by wind and cold. (For more background on kruppelholz, and the different krummholz, see p. 286 of Ben Gadd's *Handbook of the Canadian Rockies, second edition*, Corax Press, Jasper, Alberta, 1995.)

The steady descent along the drainage of Snow Creek passes a 1989 prescribed burn. There are two side trails, to Grouse Lake and to Harrison Lake, before reaching the Panther River. This is a formidable obstacle at high water. The *Upper Panther River* and *Lower Panther River* trails leave from near here, running upstream to North Fork Pass and down toward the park boundary.

South of the large warden service Windy Cabin, the trail ascends beside Wigmore Creek to the small lake at its head, then travels on an almost level stretch for nearly 3 km through a meadow. This area supports the wildflower Jacob's ladder, a member of the phlox family whose Latin species name means "very handsome," which is appropriate for the lavender blossoms complimented by yellow centres.

The side trails to Cuthead Lake and Bighorn Lake lead to places that few see. Just south of the third downstream crossing of Cuthead Creek, accomplished via a culvert, there is a shortcut to Flints Park (this junction at grid reference 913992 may be marked by a pile of stones). This is mainly used by horse parties and hasn't yet been hiked by the author. A little farther downstream, at km 43.2, is a meadow that was the site of "Cuthead College" as it was called: a training centre for park wardens in the 1950s and 1960s. There is very little evidence left.

Almost 2 km below the final crossing of Cuthead Creek, reach the junction with the *Flints Park* trail. The last section to Stony Creek and the north end of the *Lower Cascade Valley* trail travels below knolls and serrated grey ridges of the Palliser Range. The high meadows are excellent elk range and also habitat for bighorn sheep and grizzly bears.

Along the way might be sighted a creature often mentioned in contrast to grizzly bears: the hummingbird. The calliope is the smallest hummer and the smallest bird in Canada, weighing on average a mere 2.5 grams (less than one-tenth of an ounce). In this species, which is rare in Banff National Park, the males have a gorget of throat feathers that shines brilliant purple when seen in the right light.

Serpentine course of Wigmore Creek.

191

Tyrrell Creek

Distance: 11.3 km (7.0 mi) — Red Deer River to headwaters of Tyrrell Creek
Day hike/backpack: 3—3.5 hours one way
Elevation gain: 585 m (1920 ft)
Elevation loss: 20 m (65 ft)
Maximum elevation: 2270 m (7445 ft)
Maps: NTS 1:50,000 Barrier Mountain 82-O/12 and Forbidden Creek 82-O/13
Trailhead: Km 6.4 of *Upper Cascade Valley* trail (see p. 189).

0.0 — Unmarked junction (elevation 1705 m). The first bit of this trail is not well defined; staying on the east side of the creek saves a ford. Head northwest over flats toward mouth of gorge.
0.9 — Pick up trail on east side of gorge and climb to terrace. Head northwest above creek.
2.0 — High point (1815 m). Descend into small gorge of tributary stream.
2.2 — Cross tributary stream (1795 m) and climb back up to terrace. Continue upvalley, climbing steadily.
11.3 — Headwaters of Tyrrell Creek (2270 m) and Banff National Park boundary. Trail descends north to Forbidden Creek.

This side trip off the *Upper Cascade Valley* trail passes through excellent habitat for elk and bighorn sheep. There is no well-defined trail until pick up a path leading to the top of the terrace near the start.

At the base of the terrace, in an out-of-the-way spot, is the grave of a woman from Sundre who died here in 1928. According to the memorial, she was just 52 and had raised 11 children; she passed away while accompanying a daughter and a son-in-law on a trail ride.

The southwest-facing slopes above much of Tyrrell Creek are open and well-drained; here, on the first day of June, 1991, the author observed a common poorwill—which may have been the first recorded sighting of that species in Banff National Park. The small, nighthawk-like bird flushed off the ground from only about a metre away and quickly flew out of sight, but details immediately written into a journal enabled the identification.

Continuing up Tyrrell Creek toward its headwaters and the park boundary gives glimpses into several tributary valleys that invite exploration...particularly the northwesternmost one, backed by steep cliffs of the Mt. Tyrrell massif.

As returning on this outing there are views south to the Bare Range on the other side of the Red Deer River.

Wildflowers such as prairie crocus, rock jasmine, cinquefoils, and fleabanes bloom here earlier than in most areas of the park. On the debit side, ticks occur here, so do a check after an outing (see p. 23). Watch out for grizzly bears too.

Elkhorn Summit

Distance: 12.5 km (7.8 mi) — Red Deer River to Panther River
Backpack: 3.5—4 hours one way
Elevation gain: 540 m (1770 ft)
Elevation loss: 430 m (1410 ft)
Maximum elevation: 2200 m (7215 ft)
Map: NTS 1:50,000 Barrier Mountain 82-O/12
Trailhead: Km 6.4 of *Upper Cascade Valley* trail (see p. 189).

0.0 — Unmarked junction (elevation 1705 m). Head south toward Red Deer River.

0.1 — Challenging ford of Red Deer River to south bank. Begin steep climb through forest.

4.2 — Veer right to ascend low ridge; to left is an alternate route to the *Lower Panther River* trail. (This faint path heads southeast down drainage through meadows, turning east where it connects with the outlet from Elkhorn Lake. Some 700 metres downstream, climb southeast away from the creek—this vague intersection may be marked by a cairn—and follow an undulating course to reach a saddle at grid reference 922184. Descend to southwest and climb over spur ridge to arrive at top of grassy slope above Panther River. Descend steeply to *Lower Panther River* trail at km 8.6.)

4.7 — High point (2140 m) on low ridge. Head southeast.

5.6 — Elkhorn Lake (2095 m) and campsites. Climb to south.

7.0 — High point (2200 m). Descend drainage to southeast, gradually at first, then more steeply.

12.5 — Intersection (1815 m) with *Lower Panther River* trail at km 6.0.

The trail to the vast meadows known as Elkhorn Summit—situated between the Red Deer and Panther rivers east of the Bare Range—starts opposite the confluence of Tyrrell Creek and the Red Deer River.

Fording the Red Deer can be a challenging task, especially (cont. p. 194)

Grizzly bear print in muddy trail, with author's knife for scale.

(cont. from p. 193) during the snow melt: it's recommended to do this trail late in the season. The first section leads steadily up through forest. Then break into the open, where the main trail leads south over a low ridge to small Elkhorn Lake.

The main trail then climbs over a saddle and heads down to the *Lower Panther River* trail at km 6.0. En route it passes through an area of forest burned by park wardens under prescribed conditions in 1990. That there is lots of life here was reinforced for the author by surprising a boreal owl, which flew out of sight but reappeared to swoop down and capture a small rodent before disappearing into the trees...all this happening at midday.

An alternative, fainter trail to the Panther leads southeast from km 4.2, following a drainage through meadows to 500 metres east of Elkhorn Lake and downstream for another 700 metres before cutting southeast up the hillside (possible cairn of large stones marking the junction). This at-times vague route, which avoids a narrow canyon, traverses to the saddle at grid reference 922184.

The last section of this option climbs a low ridge before descending steeply from near a small pond over grassy slopes to the *Lower Panther River* trail at km 8.6. There is no established path for this last bit; if hiking this trail in the opposite direction, pick up this route by heading up through the gap some 250 metres east of the cold sulphur spring.

The author in the high meadows on the *Elkhorn Summit* trail.

Upper Panther River

Distance: 12.6 km (7.8 mi) — *Upper Cascade Valley* trail to North Fork Pass
Backpack: 3.5—4 hours one way
Elevation gain: 585 m (1920 ft)
Elevation loss: 35 m (115 ft)
Maximum elevation: 2425 m (7955 ft)
Maps: Gem Trek 1:100,000 Banff & Mt. Assiniboine and NTS 1:50,000 Barrier Mountain 82-O/12 and Castle Mountain 82-O/5
Trailhead: Km 30.0 of *Upper Cascade Valley* trail (see p. 189).

0.0 — Sign (elevation 1875 m). Head west.
0.5 — Ford Panther River to north bank and campsite. Head upvalley through wide meadows on trail that is vague at times.
5.2 — Ford Panther River to south bank. Climb southwest over shoulder.
6.9 — High point (2035 m). Descend toward river.
7.5 — Ford Panther River (2020 m) to west bank.
8.6 — Ford Panther River to east bank.
10.4 — Enter forest and climb over low shoulder.
10.9 — High point on shoulder (2185 m). Descend gradually.
11.3 — Enter drainage (2165 m) north of North Fork Pass. Follow faint path up west side of drainage, then climb steep, well-defined switchbacks toward pass.
12.6 — North Fork Pass (2425 m). The *North Cascade River* trail descends to south.

This trail starts auspiciously with a view of Panther Falls and a reasonably straightforward ford of the river to an outfitter's campsite. Then travel through a broad valley bottom with open views thanks to extensive meadows—though if the dwarf birch and other shrubs that arch over the trail are wet, no gear will stay dry.

A possible complexity on this trip is the maze of horse and elk trails, which can lead to confusion if on foot and trying to stay on route while at the same time avoiding unnecessary fords. The best is to muddle on through, keeping generally south after the pronounced bend in the river at km 6.9. Then head into forest to climb over a shoulder and drop into the tributary that leads steeply to North Fork Pass.

The directions above may sound vague, but that's the nature of this route. It should be clear that this outing is for those who like to rough it and who have a good nose for trail-finding and navigation. (The same holds for the *North Cascade River* trail on the south side of the pass, see p. 200.)

Lower Panther River

Distance: 12.2 km (7.6 mi) — *Upper Cascade Valley* trail to junction with
Panther—Dormer Divide trail
Backpack: 3—3.5 hours one way
Elevation loss: 120 m (395 ft)
Elevation gain: 15 m (50 ft)
Maximum elevation: 1875 m (6150 ft)
Map: NTS 1:50,000 Barrier Mountain 82-O/12
Trailhead: Km 30.2 of *Upper Cascade Valley* trail (see p. 189).

0.0 — Sign (elevation 1875 m) on east bank of Wigmore Creek. Head east past warden cabin and through corral and fenced meadow.

1.5 — Ford Panther River to north bank: first of three fords in 700 metres as pass through a narrow gap in the Bare Range. (A new section of trail was created on the stretch below these fords following a prescribed burn in 1990.)

4.4 — Travel through wide meadows.

5.9 — Campsite. Cross tributary.

6.0 — Keep straight (1815 m); *Elkhorn Summit* trail to left. [The trail between this point and km 8.6 may be re-routed to the south side of the river, entailing two more fords.]

8.4 — Pass cold sulphur springs.

8.6 — Keep straight at unmarked junction with faint path to left: the south end of alternative route to/from Elkhorn Summit.

8.8 — Keep straight (1795 m); horse trail fords Panther River to south bank. Follow narrow path on terrace above river.

10.0 — High point (1810 m) on terrace.

10.8 — Descend to north bank of Panther River and continue along north side.

11.2 — Rejoin horse trail.

12.1 — Ford Panther River to south bank.

12.2 — Sign at junction (1770 m) with north end of *Panther—Dormer Divide* trail. Trail down Panther River reaches Banff National Park boundary in 3 km.

The lower part of the Panther Valley within Banff National Park supports a wide variety of wildlife. It provides habitat for, among other species, bighorn sheep, elk, grizzly bear, and cougar. Among the bird species reported from this area are golden eagle, peregrine falcon, and red-eyed vireo (the latter two are rare in the park).

Starting downstream through the large meadows east of the corral at Windy Cabin, soon pass through a gap in the Bare Range. Here there are three fords of the Panther River in less than 1 km. After safely done with those, the going is straightforward along the north bank. The trail is well-marked where it passes through an area that was part of a 1990 prescribed burn.

There is a campsite on the west side of the creek shortly before the junction with the *Elkhorn Summit* trail at km 6.0. All that remains of an old trapper's cabin on the terrace just north of the campsite is a bed of ashes.

At km 8.4 are the highest known sulphur springs in the southern Canadian

Panther River; Bare Range in distance.

Rockies; these ones are cold. A more heavily travelled horse trail crosses to the south bank of the Panther 400 metres east of the springs; staying on the north side precludes at least four fords. There is a narrow but fairly well-defined game path that stays more-or-less on a contour high above the river.

Stay on the north side when the game path comes down to the river, and take game trails until intersect the horse trail. (If headed upstream, keep on the north side at the first horse crossing above the ford from the *Panther—Dormer Divide* trail, and—where hit the river again—cast around in shrubs for the trail up to the terrace.)

An easily skirted wash-out doesn't count in the above calculation of fords...it comes some 300 metres upstream of the *Panther—Dormer Divide* junction. Although a trail continues downstream from the intersection to the park boundary in 3 km, most backpackers will use the connector to the south.

As can be gathered by the above rather convoluted description, navigating on this trail—as on most front ranges trails—involves considerable mapreading and common sense.

The wilderness character of the Lower Panther River is epitomized by the presence of a wolf den; members of the pack may be heard howling.

Panther—Dormer Divide

Distance: 6.0 km (3.7 mi) — Panther River to Dormer River
Backpack: 2—2.5 hours one way
Elevation gain: 300 m (985 ft)
Elevation loss: 305 m (1000 ft)
Maximum elevation: 2060 m (6755 ft)
Map: NTS 1:50,000 Barrier Mountain 82-O/12
Trailhead: East end of *Lower Panther River* trail at km 12.2 (see p. 196).

0.0 — Sign (elevation 1770 m). Climb steadily to south.
0.5 — Cross to east side of creek.
3.0 — Saddle (2050 m). Continue south (don't descend southeast into drainage) and drop slightly.
3.2 — Low point (2040 m). Rise gradually to south.
3.6 — Panther—Dormer Divide (2060 m). Descend to south.
4.2 — Cross tributary and descend gradually to south (don't descend southeast into drainage).
6.0 — Junction (1765 m) with end of *Dormer Pass and River* trail at km 25.4.

    This short trail serves as a connector between the Panther and Dormer rivers. It is a steady haul through forest and meadows up from the Panther River to the divide. The last stretch before dropping to the Dormer River leads through open slopes interspersed with stands of trembling aspen.

    This trail ends on the north side of the Dormer, contrary to what some maps may show.

White-tailed ptarmigan.

Flints Park

Distance: 8.1 km (5.0 mi) — *Upper Cascade Valley* trail to Flints Park junction
Backpack: 2—2.5 hours one way
Elevation gain: 85 m (280 ft)
Maximum elevation: 1820 m (5970 ft)
Maps: Gem Trek 1:100,000 Banff & Mt. Assiniboine and NTS 1:50,000 Castle Mountain 82-O/5
Trailhead: Km 46.4 of *Upper Cascade Valley* trail (see p. 189).

0.0 — Sign (elevation 1735 m). Head northwest on old road.
0.3 — Cross Cuthead Creek on footbridge and keep straight; warden cabin off to right.
4.0 — Keep straight; shortcut from km 42.5 of *Upper Cascade Valley* trail comes in from northeast.
4.5 — Keep straight; outfitter's camp down to left.
7.8 — Backcountry campground. Cross footbridge to west bank of North Cascade River.
8.1 — Junction (1820 m) with east end of *Badger Pass* trail at km 17.5; *North Cascade River* trail to north and *Forty Mile Creek* trail to south.

This generally level trail grants views of the north end of the Brewster massif and of the precipitous east face of Flints Peak. Take care not to be led astray by the more well-defined trail branching left to a horse outfitter's camp at km 4.5.

Proceeding west, pass close to the base of the south cliffs of Flints Peak. Mountain goats might be sighted on the steep grey limestone slabs; a curious high-walled, small diameter log stockade nearby was used to hold some of those animals that had been captured for reintroduction to South Dakota (a disjunct part of their distribution range).

There is a backcountry campground on the east side of the North Cascade River, which is crossed to the end of this trail near the Flints Park warden cabin. This is an important four-way intersection (no stop signs, though): from here trails lead to Badger Pass, North Fork Pass, and Forty Mile Summit.

Cascade River near Flints Park; peaks near Sawback Lake in distance.

North Cascade River

Distance: 9.6 km (6.0 mi) — Flints Park to North Fork Pass
Backpack: 3—3.5 hours one way
Elevation gain: 605 m (1985 ft)
Maximum elevation: 2425 m (7955 ft)
Maps: Gem Trek 1:100,000 Banff & Mt. Assiniboine and NTS 1:50,000 Castle Mountain 82-O/5
Trailhead: End of *Flints Park* trail at km 8.1 (see p. 199). [This point can also be reached via the *Badger Pass* and *Forty Mile Creek* trails.]

0.0 — Sign (elevation 1820 m). Take old road north for 50 metres, then turn left up faint path.

0.2 — Turn right where join wide graded track coming up from west off *Badger Pass* trail.

2.8 — Ford North Cascade River to east bank. Continue north upvalley, on wide graded track at first, later on indistinct path through meadows.

5.7 — Ford North Cascade River to west bank.

6.2 — Ford North Cascade River to east bank and begin climbing steep switchbacking trail to north.

7.3 — Trail levels out and traverses above northernmost tributary of North Cascade River.

8.4 — Cross tributary. Trail disappears: proceed up slope to north.

9.3 — Rejoin established path and climb gently toward pass.

9.6 — North Fork Pass (2425 m) at grid reference 826034 {may be unmarked on topo map}. *Upper Panther River* trail descends to north.

The trail up this remote valley from Flints Park provides a challenging outing for experienced backpackers. This area is known for its concentration of grizzly bears: park warden Diane Volkers once had five in view south of North Fork Pass.

The going is easy for the first 2.8 km. Beyond the ford to the east side of the North Cascade River, however, the route becomes sketchy. At first it is on an old logging road with many log cribs that were used in a salvage operation after a forest fire. But the road eventually fades and it can be hard to keep to the faint path through meadows.

The trail becomes clearer as it climbs out of the valley to get above the trees, switchbacking high before contouring to the northernmost tributary of the river. Remaining on the east side of that stream, it rises into a northeast-trending valley and then crosses the stream before heading up an open slope.

Here the trail becomes ambiguous again, but the notch of North Fork Pass is obvious. Climbing up through low vegetation will lead to within sight of the saddle and onto a faint trail once more.

North Fork Pass permits sweeping views, including back south to the peaks of the Sawback Range and beyond. On the north side of the pass is the *Upper Panther River* trail, an equally demanding wilderness outing.

Dormer Pass and River

Distance: 25.4 km (15.7 mi) — *Lower Cascade Valley* trail to south end of *Panther—Dormer Divide* trail
Backpack: 1.5—2 days one way
Elevation gain: 730 m (2395 ft)
Elevation loss: 605 m (1985 ft)
Maximum elevation: 2355 m (7725 ft)
Maps: Gem Trek 1:100,000 Banff & Mt. Assiniboine and NTS 1:50,000 Castle Mountain 82-O/5 and Barrier Mountain 82-O/12
Trailhead: North end of *Lower Cascade Valley* trail at km 15.2 (see p. 60).

0.0 — Sign (elevation 1640 m). Head east.
0.3 — Backcountry campground. Trail cuts up steeply to terrace above Stony Creek.
0.9 — High point (1685 m). Descend toward creek.
1.3 — Ford Stony Creek (1670 m) to east bank and head north up valley.
2.0 — Ford tributary.
6.5 — Ford Stony Creek to west bank
6.6 — Cross tributary (possible rockhop).
7.0 — Ford Stony Creek to east bank.
9.0 — Keep straight (1955 m); *Stony Creek—Dormer River Headwaters* trail to right.
9.1 — Ford Stony Creek to north bank. Begin steep ascent.
12.7 — Dormer Pass (2355 m). Descend steeply, to northwest at first.
17.2 — Trail levels out in valley of Dormer River.
18.7 — Keep straight and ford Dormer River to east bank; warden cabin to left. (cont. p. 202)

The author in Dormer Pass.

(cont. from p. 201)
18.8 — Turn left (1925 m); *Stony Creek—Dormer River Headwaters* trail to right. Cross tributary and head downvalley at gentle grade, passing through large meadows.
25.0 — Ford Dormer River to west bank.
25.4 — Cross tributary to junction (1765 m). *Panther—Dormer Divide* trail to left; Banff National Park boundary 6 km to right.

Working up the narrow valley of Stony Creek, hemmed in between steep ramparts of the Palliser Range, there are several fords required to reach the region of Dormer Pass. There are also some steep sections before the pass.

The effort is well worthwhile both for the high, open country reached and for abundant wildlife. The Dormer Pass area supports bighorn sheep, mountain goats, and elk; the latter visit the alpine meadows in winter, the evidence being cast antlers. (Note that all antlers should be left undisturbed; for one thing, they are an important source of calcium for certain rodents.) The cast elk antlers confirm that, as shown by studies in Banff National Park, their movement patterns are variable: not all of them follow the general rule of "high in summer, low in winter."

The entire length of this trail—indeed, all of the front ranges—is also prime habitat for grizzly bears. The author can attest to this, having been treed by a subadult just 500 metres from the Stony Creek backcountry campground in June, 1989. Out of curiosity, the bear climbed up too, which puts to rest the false notion that grizzlies don't climb (full-grown adults usually can't manage to get very high because of their weight).

Luckily, the nearby lodgepole pine that the author went up was tall enough to enable him to clamber into the crown and above the branches that could support the bear's weight (although it did come up to within one metre). The author considers himself responsible for this episode since he had temporarily neglected to make noise to warn bears of his presence; for excellent information on the subject of bears and safety, consult Dr. S. Herrero's *Bear Attacks: Their Causes and Avoidance.*

The Dormer Pass area is good for wildflowers. Among those that can be found in bloom are rock jasmine, larkspur, forget-me-not, moss campion, and a species with the rather ominous name of scorpionweed—it has a beautiful yellow-tipped purple spike of flowers.

The open expanses of the pass are an ideal area for sighting the horned lark, a bird species in which the male has two small projections on its head.

If have extra energy, it is recommended to explore the knoll south of the pass [grid reference 997987], particularly for the views it grants of the rugged surroundings. Otherwise, the trail descends steeply north to a tributary of the Dormer River...oddly, Dormer Pass is not at the headwaters of the main branch of the river (see *Stony Creek —Dormer River Headwaters* trail description on page opposite).

After the ford at km 18.7, the trail stays on the east bank, alternately through forest and over open flats, until another crossing of the Dormer at km 25.0. A rockhop or ford of a small creek 400 metres farther leads to the junction with the *Panther— Dormer Divide* trail. This is the most likely route if continuing onward; a trail does continue downstream on the Dormer to the park boundary in 6 km.

Stony Creek—Dormer River Headwaters

Distance: 13.8 km (8.6 mi) — Connector over Stony Creek—Dormer River divide
Backpack: 4—4.5 hours one way
Elevation gain: 375 m (1230 ft)
Elevation loss: 405 m (1330 ft)
Maximum elevation: 2330 m (7640 ft)
Maps: Gem Trek 1:100,000 Banff & Mt. Assiniboine and NTS 1:50,000 Castle Mountain 82-O/5
Trailhead: Km 9.0 of *Dormer Pass and River* trail (see p. 201).

0.0 — Sign (elevation 1955 m). Climb steadily up drainage to east on narrow path.
0.5 — Cross tributary.
3.5 — Cross Stony Creek to north bank. Break out into meadows.
5.7 — Saddle (2330 m) between headwaters of Stony Creek and those of Divide River. Descend to north.
7.0 — Cross Dormer River to east bank (possible rockhop). Descend valley on steady grade through shrubby meadows.
13.8 — Junction (1925 m) with *Dormer Pass and River* trail at km 18.8.

Only the committed few try this seldom-used trail: when the author met park warden Larry Gilmar on patrol in this area in 1989, he was told that probably fewer than 10 people a year go this way on foot.

The trail climbs steeply through forest parallel to Stony Creek before breaking out into meadows among unnamed jagged grey limestone peaks. The route can be confusing where it passes through high shrubs, but the watershed saddle at grid reference 036984 is obvious.

Three tiny pools sit in the pass; a very few subalpine larch occur in the high valleys. Despite the marginal conditions, there is a variety of flora present, including gentians, cinquefoils, chickweed, and forget-me-not. Look for pikas and white-tailed ptarmigan feeding on the vegetation.

The trail makes a long, gradual descent down the main branch of the Dormer, and is heavily overgrown with dwarf birch. The stuff is only a little less abrasive than sandpiper, so shorts are not recommended as hiking through it.

Detail of cliff seen from *Stony Creek—Dormer River Headwaters* trail.

Notes